My Magical Trip to Ireland

Mica Boyd Johnston

DEDICATION

This book is dedicated to my ancestors—those courageous and adventurous souls who crossed vast oceans and traversed thousands of miles, enduring hardships and overcoming challenges. Their resilience and spirit live on in me, shaping the adventurer I am today.

THREADS ACROSS THE SEA

Embarking on a trip to Ireland,

A mix of joy and apprehension.

The Emerald Isle, with its myths and legends,

Stories so old beyond my comprehension.

Untold adventures await,

Building those memories, I leave them to fate.

I've researched and read that the stars and stripes in my soul,

Will be met with glaring, icy cold.

"Beware the welcomes cold,

For those who hail from the land of the Bold."

Ireland and America share an enduring connection,

Freedom rings are Ireland's reflection.

But has the distance torn us apart?

And when did that exactly start?

Across the sea, two nations shared,

Dreams of freedom if we dared.

We fought together for a common goal,

Both proud hearts were pounding bold.

In every Irish melody,

Lies an echo of the free.

In America's tapestry,

A thread of green, you'll see.

Let's honor the bonds that history designed,

When once we were woven of the same vine.

TABLE OF CONTENTS

CHAPTER ONE: YEARNING

For as long as I can remember, I've always wanted to go to Ireland. Ireland was more than a distant dream—it was a yearning, a pull deep within my soul that I couldn't shake. I don't know where it came from, maybe a story overheard as a child or a scene from an old television program, but whatever it was, it became an essential part of me. I felt some type of connection with Ireland, and I wanted to know why. The longing I felt ran deeper than simple curiosity—it pulsed like an inherited memory as if my soul were tracing its own roots. No one in my family shared this relentless yearning, but I knew it had to be ancestral, a call from something ancient within me. So, when I launched into my ancestry research, I had one certainty: I had to have Irish blood. My fair skin, red hair, freckles, and love for storytelling seemed to echo a heritage I had yet to uncover.

After nearly 25 years of painstaking ancestry research, that relentless pursuit finally led me to a direct connection. The day I found my Irish roots in official documents was nothing short of life-changing. It felt as if the world held its breath, and in that stillness, I was transformed. I had pushed, researched, and written countless letters over the years, but at that moment, as I uncovered my heritage, I could finally declare it to the world: I was undeniably, truly Irish. Five generations back, hidden in the archives of time, lay my heritage, and discovering it filled me with an indescribable joy. It was the moment I had waited my whole life for, and it was exhilarating.

From that day on, my Irish descent wasn't just a fact—it became a core part of who I was. I started wearing my red hair and freckles with a new sense of pride. And whenever someone called me "Red," I couldn't help but smile, knowing deep down that I was carrying the spirit of Ireland with me everywhere I went.

The discovery filled me with a surge of curiosity and pride. It felt as if I had uncovered a missing piece of myself, a puzzle I hadn't realized needed completing. That revelation ignited a deeper drive to explore Irish traditions, sparking a hope that maybe some of the customs I grew up with were tied to my Irish roots.

At the beginning of my research, there was no internet; my search for answers relied on handwritten letters and the long, uncertain wait for a response—if a response ever came. For twenty-five years, I wrote to strangers, mailing letters to unknown addresses, each one carrying my hope for a clue. Every response, or lack thereof, left me in suspense for months. I spent endless hours researching, combing through whatever I could find on Ireland, and talking to every relative I knew. Every family dinner or reunion I spent asking questions from anyone who would talk. From my parents and their siblings to long-lost cousins, I asked questions, hoping for any detail that might lead me closer to my roots. What surprised me most was how little many of the older generations knew about their ancestry. It was as if time had quietly erased the stories, leaving me to piece them back together, letter by letter.

During my research, I came to a heartbreaking realization: many families, especially those separated by vast distances and oceans, often lost touch with each other, sometimes forever. In times past, when long-distance travel meant crossing continents or seas and communication relied on slow mail or word of mouth, families would say goodbye, knowing they might never see or hear from each other again. The emotional toll of these separations was immense, as the bonds that once held them together frayed with time and distance.

As generations passed, these lost connections meant stories, traditions, and even the memory of family roots could fade away. The longer people were separated, the more difficult it became to bridge that gap, and eventually, details about entire branches of a family tree would simply vanish. This was a sobering thought in the early stages of my search, knowing that I was trying to reclaim pieces of history that had been lost to time and circumstance.

I often wonder about the countless families who left their homes behind to seek a new life in another country. How many were torn apart by famine, slavery, or political upheaval? How many cherished memories and stories were lost across the generations, swallowed by the passage of time? It's a sobering thought—how much of humanity's shared history has slipped through our fingers, leaving us with only fragments of the lives and legacies of those who came before us.

Despite the challenges of knowing I may never know the real history of my ancestry, I kept moving forward. I did uncover a few wonderful details about some of my ancestors—stories and facts that no one in my family had known. Thankfully, some of these stories were written in newspaper articles and books. Each discovery felt like a small victory against the forces of distance and time, bringing those lost connections back into the light. It was exciting to find a small piece of family history and to share that information with my family. The conversations would start up amongst the family when given a new piece of information to ponder. My mother's sisters would start a three-way call and talk for hours. One sister, Sybil, lived in L.A., while the other sister, Sadie, lived in Windsor Locks, Connecticut, and my mom lived in Midland, Texas. Those three would talk for hours about whatever new information I found. It brought me immense joy to listen to their conversations because not only were they so happy talking about childhood memories, but it gave me more insight as to where to look next.

I began my research in the early 1990s, driven by an unshakable yearning deep in my soul—a need to know my roots that felt impossible to fill. It became the force behind everything I did, the driving energy that pushed me to search for answers. I made plans to visit Ireland several times, but life always seemed to intervene. A child would fall ill, a family member needed help, or I had to move or start a new job. There was never enough time, and money always seemed too tight. Eventually, I stopped planning altogether, but the yearning never left me.

Back in the '90s, travel planning was still mostly done through travel agents, but that wasn't what I wanted. I didn't just want a pre-packaged tour; I wanted to explore every corner of Ireland on my own terms, walk where my ancestors walked, and discover hidden places connected to my family. But with the internet in its infancy, there was little information available to plan a trip like that. It felt like an impossible task, and as the years went by, my dream of visiting Ireland began to fade slowly, swallowed by the realities of life. Yet the desire in my heart—the deep, aching need to connect with my heritage—never really went away.

As I grew older and life began to settle down, I felt a familiar longing resurface—the dreams of my youth that I had set aside for so long. Chief among them was the desire to visit Ireland, a dream that had never truly left me. Though buried deep, it still smoldered within me, like embers quietly waiting to be reignited. What rekindled that flame was the rise of the modern internet. Suddenly, the world opened up in ways I had never imagined. The internet became an invaluable tool for both my ancestry research and travel planning. It allowed me to uncover family history and map out my dream trip with ease. With each new discovery, my excitement grew, and the dream that had once seemed out of reach felt more possible than ever.

In 2023, I took a spontaneous trip to Scotland with my best friend, Christina McKinney, through a tour company. Although I didn't have the opportunity to dive into my ancestry while there, I felt an incredible sense of belonging among the people. Knowing that my dad's family had Scottish roots, I was beyond thrilled to experience the land firsthand. It was more than just a vacation—it felt like coming home.

The journey to Scotland deepened my desire to visit Ireland. Even though Scotland and Ireland are different in many ways, my mother always told me we were Scotch Irish, and that connection lingered in my mind. In the beginning, I wasn't sure what Scotch Irish meant. I had found my ancestral connection to Ireland, but I was unable to trace my roots to Scotland at that time. I knew the Boyd Surname originated in Scotland, but I couldn't find the documentation that took the family from Scotland to Ireland. I did, however, have official documents that took my ancestral line from the States back to Ireland, so this is what I focused on. As soon as I returned to the States, I knew I had to plan a trip to Ireland—come hell or high water, I was going to make it happen.

In 2024, I started seriously planning my trip to Ireland. The desire to see the lush green landscapes, feel the ocean air on my skin and walk on that ancient soil burned within me stronger than any wish I'd ever had. There was nothing I craved more. Those early stages of planning were thrilling—a journey of their own, filled with excitement and the promise of adventure. I longed to walk the path of my ancestors and wondered if I would feel a connection to the land.

I joined a variety of social media groups and forums dedicated to all things Ireland—communities focused on travel experiences, advice for exploring the country, and tips for planning the perfect trip. Whether it was recommendations on where to stay, what to see, or the best ways to immerse myself in Irish culture, I wanted to learn everything I could before setting off on my journey.

I spent the next few months planning, then changing those plans and planning again. I saw so many places I wanted to visit and so many sites that I knew I had to experience. Ireland had so much to offer, and figuring out which sites to visit and which sites I would have to skip would become daunting, to say the least.

During my intensive research, I stumbled upon a social media page that completely broke my heart and almost changed my plans for the trip to Ireland. An American woman had asked about visiting the Temple Bar in Dublin, wondering if it was too touristy or better suited for a younger crowd. The responses were quick and cruel, filled with harsh criticism about Americans. Many of those comments came from Irish people themselves, and even some Americans chimed in to say that most of their fellow citizens were arrogant, apologizing for their behavior. What hurt most was the underlying message: the Irish people strongly disliked it when Americans claimed Irish ancestry. "No, you are not Irish. You are American," they said, rejecting a connection that many of us use to identify ourselves. It felt like a door slamming shut on my sense of belonging.

And then came the words that truly made my heart ache: an Irish man boldly declared that it would be better if all Americans stopped calling themselves Irish—and stopped coming to Ireland altogether. It was as if a piece of my dream was suddenly taken away, and all the excitement I had felt for this trip and who I was was dimmed by the weight of rejection.

That beautiful sense of belonging to a culture so rich in tradition and history was suddenly ripped away from me. It felt like the ground beneath my feet had been pulled out, leaving me with a hollow ache. For so long, I had carried this connection to Ireland like a cherished heirloom—something precious, deeply rooted, and unbreakable. But now, it felt fragile, almost counterfeit, as if I had no right to claim it at all.

Post after post was filled with sharp remarks and thinly veiled hostility toward Americans. Discussions about tourists would quickly spiral into criticisms of Americans being too loud, too entitled, or too clueless. Even when someone asked an innocent question about visiting a particular site, it wasn't uncommon for the responses to drip with sarcasm or irritation.

I tried to brush it off, telling myself it was just a handful of angry voices in an otherwise warm and welcoming community. But then it happened again—and again. Even the typically kind Canadians couldn't help but share their frustrations, recounting encounters with "those Americans" who apparently embarrassed themselves at every turn.

Each comment felt like a small jab, chipping away at the excitement I had been carrying. Did they hate us? Did they roll their eyes when someone said, *"My great-grandmother came from Ireland"* or *"I've always felt connected to Ireland"*? Was it so annoying to hear Americans claim Irish ancestry, even if it came from a place of genuine pride and curiosity?

I felt lost and disheartened. I hadn't even set foot in Ireland yet, and already I felt unwelcome. My enthusiasm for planning this trip—something I had dreamed about for years—was now clouded by doubt and insecurity. Would I show up and be instantly labeled as just another clueless American? Would every smile I received feel forced, every interaction tinged with unspoken judgment?

But deep down, I also recognized the source of these frustrations. I had seen those stereotypical tourists myself—the ones who treated travel like a checklist rather than an opportunity to connect, the ones who expected every place to cater to their needs rather than respecting local customs. I understood why those stories circulated. But it still hurt to feel lumped into that category before I'd even arrived.

At that moment, I had to remind myself why I wanted to visit Ireland in the first place. It wasn't to prove anything to anyone, nor was it to claim ownership over a culture I had only ever admired from afar. It was to learn, to listen, and to honor the roots that had been passed down to me.

I unfollowed countless social media pages, turning away from the negativity and searching elsewhere to plan my trip, if I even continued on the trip. I found plenty of travel agencies willing to send me brochures filled with beautiful images and detailed itineraries to help me plan. But it just wasn't the same—my heart wasn't in it anymore. How could I go to a place where I felt unwelcome? The excitement I once felt for this journey was now shadowed by a lingering feeling of rejection, making it hard to imagine traveling somewhere that didn't seem to want me there.

I poured countless hours and a good part of my life into claiming my Scotch-Irish heritage. For 25 years, I researched my ancestry, determined to trace that connection, only to be told by an Irishman that I wasn't "truly Irish." It shattered me. Did they not understand how deeply we hold onto these identities and how much they mean to us? Identity is something intimate, something that roots us, and hearing those words from him broke something in me. It felt as if my heritage, the years of devotion, the pride I'd carried—it was all dismissed in an instant. I was left feeling as if the very soul I'd worked so hard to reclaim had been taken from me.

Then, my friend Christina invited me to the St. Patrick's Day party at our local bar. I was hesitant to go, considering how I felt, but I pushed myself to go. When I arrived, the atmosphere was lively and full of Irish cheer. There was a man playing the bagpipes in a traditional kilt, the bar was decorated with party favors themed around all things Ireland, and the green beer was flowing. People from all walks of life were here celebrating all things Irish and having a great time. I saw all this Irish cheer but could only think about the words of the Irish man, "You are not Irish. You are American." I wondered if these Americans knew how the Irish really felt about us Americans.

I wove through the crowded bar, the words I'd read on social media still circling in my mind as I searched for Christina. I finally spotted her, laughing with a stranger, her hand wrapped around a full mug of green beer. She wore a leprechaun hat and oversized green sunglasses, fully embracing the festive chaos. Watching her charm the stranger, I couldn't help but think she could pass for Irish with how effortlessly she made friends. She spotted me, her face lighting up with a big smile. Pulling me into a warm hug, she handed me her mug of green beer and exclaimed, "You made it! Now you have to catch up!"

As the beer flowed, my initial uncertainty about being there began to fade. Christina and I spent the next few hours laughing and chatting with new and old friends, the lively energy of the evening sweeping us along. As the night wore on, we shared our plans for a trip to Ireland that year. People leaned in with curiosity, asking the usual questions—when, how much, and why.

Later, as the conversation shifted, I pulled Christina aside to vent my frustration. The negative comments I'd come across on social media had dimmed some of my excitement for the trip. I found myself second-guessing everything, even wondering if we should go to Ireland at all. "Maybe we should pick somewhere else," I muttered, my voice tinged with bitterness. The thought of the Irish rejecting my connection to their culture left a sour taste, making me question the journey we were so excited to take.

She listened patiently, her smile warm and her cheeks a little flushed from the drinks, then said something that completely changed my outlook: "If people can identify however feels right to them, then you absolutely can identify as Irish—or anything else that feels like home. Besides, we all know you're Irish with that red hair and those freckles!" That's when a moment of epiphany happened. She was right! I can identify however I feel. Her words were exactly what I needed to hear.

In America, identity is deeply personal. With so many cultures and histories blending here, each of us finds a unique sense of belonging that includes not only America but also distant places that feel like home to us. Christina was right; identity is ours to shape. Why hadn't I thought of that? Suddenly, my joy of visiting Ireland came flooding back. With renewed enthusiasm, I donned my festive leprechaun hat, lifted my glass, and toasted to all things Irish!

Christina's words gave me the fortitude to push past the negativity and reclaim my excitement for my heritage. It was a reminder that identity is deeply personal, and no one could take away my sense of connection to Ireland. That night renewed my confidence and gave me the push I needed to start planning my trip again, this time with more determination and joy than ever before. It reminded me that embracing my roots and following my dream to explore Ireland was something no online comment could tarnish.

As an American with Irish ancestry, I learned that Irish immigrants who left Ireland were not leaving by choice but by necessity—a heartbreaking separation from everything they knew and loved. During my research, I tended to romanticize my heritage. I learned that many Americans fall in love with their ancestral culture.

For the Irish, their identity is not a romanticized heritage but a living, breathing connection to a land scarred by struggle and resilience. Claiming that ancestry without truly grasping the weight of history might feel like reducing their pain and perseverance to a distant, diluted narrative.

For both Americans and Irish, it's a reminder that ancestry is more than a name or a place—it's the stories, the wounds, and the unbroken thread of a people's spirit.

CHAPTER TWO: TRIP PLANNING

The next day, with renewed excitement, I revisited several social media platforms to research potential sites for my trip to Ireland, again focusing on those who shared their personal travel experiences. Ignoring the negativity, I honed in on the feedback that highlighted vacation must-sees and must-dos. As a history enthusiast, I prioritized locations rich in historical significance when finalizing the itinerary.

With a long list of sites that I wanted to visit, I had to narrow it down due to time constraints. Although I would have loved to spend a month in Ireland, I only had about a week, so I carefully chose the most captivating locations. However, the first major decision I had was which city to fly into from the U.S.

After reviewing the flight options for various destinations in Ireland, it quickly became clear that flying into Dublin was the most practical and cost-effective choice. Other airports, like Shannon, Cork, and Belfast, offered fewer flights and tended to have higher fares, while Dublin had a wider range of options with more competitive pricing. The availability of direct flights and better connections made Dublin the best choice for both convenience and budget. Now, please bear in mind that all of this research was done for me personally, and things may change in the future. But for right now, flying into Dublin was the better option for me. With that settled, I obtained a map of Ireland and began marking the key sites I wanted to visit. Over the course of about four weeks, I compiled an extensive list of places to see, but given the limited one-week time limit, I had to prioritize.

My best and closest friend, Christina, was joining me, and she was bringing along her daughter, Angela. Together, we had ten days in total, with two reserved for travel, leaving us with eight days to explore as many sites as possible. During the research phase, it was important to me that I included locations that were meaningful to all of us. I made sure to talk with Christina and Angela about potential sites to ensure they aligned with their interests as well. Since this was their trip, too, I valued their input on what they liked and disliked, making sure our itinerary reflected everyone's preferences.

After about a month of back-and-forth, revising, and rethinking locations, we ultimately decided to focus solely on a trip to Southern Ireland. Unfortunately, due to time constraints, we had to cut many sites in Northern Ireland—there simply wasn't enough time to see and do everything.

I had originally intended to go to Northern Ireland, specifically Ballymena in County Tyrone, where my great-great-great-grandfather was born. My heart ached to visit this place and delve deeper into my family's history. However, I quickly realized that it wouldn't be fair to Christina and Angela, who were traveling with me, to spend the entire trip focused on my research.

I had longed to explore Northern Ireland and walk the path of my ancestors. Instead, here I was, focused on the southern half of Ireland. I knew in my heart that experiencing any part of this beautiful country would still be meaningful, and in the end, going to Ireland was better than not going. My heart ached, but I embraced the adventure that lay ahead with my friends, leaving the door open for another journey to Northern Ireland someday. Besides, according to Ancestry.com, I had cousins who lived in Dublin, so maybe I could meet up with one of them for a pint.

During the planning process, I learned something new: Ireland is actually two separate countries. Northern Ireland is part of the UK and uses pounds, while the Republic of Ireland (the bottom three-quarters of the island) is part of the EU and uses euros. So, we decided to split our plans into two trips: the first in 2024 to the Republic of Ireland and a future trip to Northern Ireland. Although it was disappointing, we realized that trying to see both in one trip would have been too rushed.

I narrowed down the list of sites in southern Ireland and allocated the days between the cities we planned to visit. Given the abundance of things to see in and around Dublin, I decided to spend four days there. Afterward, we would take the train to Galway for two days, then continue to Cork for another two nights. Finally, we would take the train back to Dublin on the day of our flight back to the U.S. This plan allowed us to cover all the key sites on the list within the available time, and it worked out perfectly. The following is the final itinerary for our 2024 trip to the Emerald Isle, including cost estimates.

FINAL ITINERARY FOR IRELAND

FRI   5/17/2024   FLY TO DALLAS

INTERNATIONAL FLIGHT LEAVES @ 6:50 PM – OVERNIGHT FLIGHT

SAT   5/18/2024   LAND IN DUBLIN @ 9:45 AM (HOTEL WILL HOLD LUGGAGE)

HARDING HOTEL 2 PM CHECK-IN

CHRIST CHURCH (ACROSS FROM HOTEL) SELF-GUIDED TOUR

ST PATRICK'S CATHEDRAL (TICKETS AT DOOR) 2-HOUR TOUR

TRINITY COLLEGE (WALKING TOUR 1 HOUR)

BOOKS OF KELLS (TOUR @ 3 PM 1 ½ HOURS) ARRIVE EARLY

TEMPLE BAR AREA – PERAMBULATION

MOLLY MALONE STATUE – PHOTO OP

HA'PENNY BRIDGE – PHOTO OP

DARKEY KELLEYS PUB – TRADITIONAL IRISH PUB

SUN   5/19/2024   SECOND NIGHT @ HARDING HOTEL

DUBLINIA MUSEUM (VIKING MUSEUM) 90 MIN TOUR @ 10 AM

HOP-ON HOP-OFF BUS TOUR

GUINNESS BREWERY (TOUR @ 3 PM) 90 MIN TOUR ARRIVE EARLY

HOP-ON HOP-OFF BUS TOUR

DARKEY KELLEYS PUB – NIGHT TWO

MON 5/20/2024   CLONTARF CASTLE

NEWGRANGE TOUR BY MARY GIBBONS – ALL-DAY TOUR

KNIGHTS BAR – DINNER AND DRINKS

TUE   5/21/2024   CLONTARF CASTLE

SEAN'S BAR (OLDEST BAR IN IRELAND) TRAIN TO ATHLONE 1 ½ HR

WALK DUBLIN BAY

WED 5/22/2024   EYRE SQUARE HOTEL IN GALWAY

TRAIN TO GALWAY 2 ½ HOURS FROM HUESTON STATION

LATIN QUARTER

QUAY STREET

SPANISH ARCH – PHOTO OP

GALWAY CITY MUSEUM

JFK BUST – PHOTO OP

THU   5/23/2024   EYRE SQUARE HOTEL IN GALWAY

CLIFFS OF MOHER – ALL-DAY TOUR

PERAMBULATION

FRI   5/24/2024   MONTENOTTE HOTEL IN CORK

LEAVE GALWAY BY TRAIN 4 HOURS

EXPLORE DOWNTOWN CORK

SAT   5/25/2024   MONTENOTTE IN CORK

BLARNEY CASTLE AND GROUNDS TOUR – 3 HOURS

PERAMBULATION

SUN   5/26/2024   FLIGHT BACK TO THE STATES

                        TAKE THE TRAIN FROM CORK TO DUBLIN – CAB TO AIRPORT

ESTIMATED COSTS

IRELAND 2024

ALL COSTS ESTIMATED FOR THREE ADULTS

AMERICAN AIRLINES ROUND TRIP	4336.10
HARDING HOTEL – TWO NIGHTS	608.62
BOOK OF KELLS TICKETS	76.38
FOOD & DRINKS DAY 1	150.00
DUBLINIA MUSEUM TICKETS	42.00
GUINNESS BREWERY TICKETS	124.40
FOOD & DRINKS DAY 2	150.00
CLONTARF CASTLE – TWO NIGHTS	908.00
NEWGRANGE TOUR TICKETS	225.00
FOOD & DRINKS DAY 3	150.00
TRAIN TO ATHLONE	60.00
TRAIN BACK TO DUBLIN	60.00
FOOD & DRINKS DAY 4	150.00
EYRE SQUARE HOTEL – TWO NIGHTS	581.14
TRAIN FROM DUBLIN TO GALWAY	75.00
FOOD & DRINKS DAY 5	150.00
CLIFFS OF MOHER TICKETS	164.31
MONTENOTTE HOTEL – TWO NIGHTS	752.66
FOOD & DRINKS DAY 6	150.00
BLARNEY CASTLE & GROUNDS TICKETS	60.00

TRAIN FROM CORK TO DUBLIN	150.00
TOTAL ESTIMATED COST	$9,123.61
DIVIDED BY THREE ADULTS	$3,041.20

CHAPTER THREE: DUBLIN

Saturday, May 18, 2024

Day 1: We arrived in Dublin at 9:45 a.m., and from the moment we deboarded, I was delighted to hear the Irish accent echoing throughout the airport. The accent is truly lovely, and I immediately felt at home. Although it took a few moments to adjust to the nuances of their English—some words are different, and certain accents are quite thick—I quickly found myself understanding with ease.

We took a taxi to our hotel, the Harding Hotel, located in the Temple Bar district. Since it was too early to check into the hotel, the hotel staff offered to watch our backpacks until we could check-in. The Harding Hotel is a charming hotel located on Fishamble Street, one of the oldest streets in Dublin. The historic ambiance of the hotel, with features like Cooper Alley running through its reception area, added a unique touch to our stay. The hotel, with its rich history, was the ideal spot for our first two nights, and it was close to many of the sites I wanted to explore. Attached to the hotel is Darkey Kelly's, a traditional Irish pub that I had come across during my research on social media. The pub was everything I hoped for, full of live music, singing, and plenty of beer flowing—a quintessential Irish experience.

Before diving into the pub experience, I have to share our first amazing day. It was truly wonderful. We walked everywhere, which was a big change from what we're used to in West Texas, where driving is the norm. All the walking was a refreshing and different experience for us.

Our first stop was Christ Church Cathedral, conveniently located right across from our hotel. I was surprised to learn that Dublin was originally a Viking settlement, and the cathedral itself was built by the Viking King Sitric Silkenbeard in 1030 A.D. Knowing my dad is a descendant of Vikings[1], that fact made the visit even more special for me. The church, with its rich history, stood tall in all its glory—a massive European structure that left us in awe.

Inside, the atmosphere was humbling. The cathedral's 19th-century bells, with the oldest dating back to 1738, range from a quarter of a ton to 2.5 tons. Christ Church even holds a world record for the number of bells available for full-circle ringing. The first recorded mention of the bell dates back to 1423, marking the death of John Kyrcham, 'maker of our bells.' It was a powerful and memorable start to our trip, immersing us in history from the very beginning.

Inside Christ Church, a choir was singing, and their voices resonated beautifully throughout the halls. The church's architecture was designed to amplify the sound, making the music feel even more powerful. The ambiance was nothing short of divine, creating an awe-inspiring, humbling experience that gave a whole new meaning to the phrase "god-like."

The Choir of Christ Church Cathedral is renowned for its extensive and diverse repertoire, encompassing over five centuries of sacred music. Their performances include traditional Anglican choral works, plainsong, and pieces from the late Renaissance period. The choir also engages with contemporary compositions, often premiering works commissioned specifically for them. The specific pieces performed can vary, and the cathedral provides a music list detailing the repertoire.

The emotional intensity of hearing the choir live is hard to put into words. Hearing the choir left us with a lasting impression—a reminder of the beauty and power of the human voice. That and the ancient setting

---

[1] Yes, I understand that 'Vikings' isn't a specific place but a term used to describe people of Norse descent, particularly those known for their seafaring, trading, and raiding activities during the Viking Age.

made the whole experience otherworldly. At that moment, we were connected to something more than ourselves—we were connected to something divine.

It was difficult to tear ourselves away from the majestic voices of the choir, their harmonies resonating and seemingly embedded in the cathedral's ancient stone walls. Yet, the allure of exploring the rest of Christ Church Cathedral beckoned us onward. As we moved along the towering interior walls, we marveled at their intricate stonework and the array of religious décor adorning them. Beautifully crafted stained-glass windows cast colorful patterns on the floor, and centuries-old paintings and carvings depicted sacred stories and figures. After soaking in the serene atmosphere of the main hall, we descended to the crypt, eager to uncover the treasures hidden below.

The basement, or as they call it, the Crypt of Christ Church Cathedral, had a cold, dimly lit atmosphere, evoking the feeling of a true medieval castle. The crypt was particularly special—not only is it Dublin's oldest functioning structure, but it's also the largest crypt in Ireland. With its ancient stone walls and 11th-century medieval architecture, it felt like stepping back in time.

We spent about two hours at Christ Church, using headsets to guide us through its rich history. I was deeply moved by the sheer amount of history we were walking through. After exploring the church, we stepped into the gardens, where I felt like the queen of Ireland. The garden was beautiful, filled with old trees, vibrant flowers, and lush bushes, creating a peaceful atmosphere.

While exploring the garden, I noticed a sign that read, *"No Mow May."* This initiative encourages leaving grass unmowed during May to allow bees and insects to thrive before their habitats are disturbed. Interestingly, I saw the same sign at many of the sites we visited that day. As a bee lover, this concept deeply resonated with me, and I brought the idea back with me to the States. It is something I will always be grateful for, as it aligns perfectly with my passion for supporting pollinators.

Although Christ Church was lively with tourists, it was not overcrowded, allowing us to fully immerse ourselves in the experience. Once we had taken in all its beauty, we stepped back into the bustling streets of Dublin. The cobbled streets were alive with the rhythm of people strolling and cars navigating the curves around the church and nearby businesses.

Just across from the church, we discovered a quaint coffee shop that felt like a hidden gem—the RoCo Café. The moment we stepped inside, the city's noise melted away, replaced by a comforting stillness. The rich aroma of freshly roasted coffee greeted us warmly, wrapping us in a sense of calm. A delightful display of freshly baked pastries tempted us, each one looking more irresistible than the last. The ambiance was cozy and inviting, with a charm that seemed uniquely Irish. We ordered lattes and blueberry scones and proceeded to find a seat next to the window.

As we sipped our lattes and watched the world pass by outside, a sense of wonder settled over me. Somehow, everything—from the rich, comforting flavors of the coffee to the warmth of the atmosphere—seemed to be imbued with a unique kind of charm. It was as though Ireland itself had woven its quiet magic into this simple moment. This moment was the magic that is Ireland.

As we stepped out of the coffee shop, the vibrant pulse of the city immediately surrounded us. The hum of activity, the chatter of passersby, and the energy of Dublin filled the air. From there, we strolled just a few blocks to St. Patrick's Cathedral, eager to embark on our next adventure.

St. Patrick's Cathedral is one of the most iconic landmarks in Ireland. Its beauty and grandeur humbled me. It is the largest cathedral in the country and serves as the national cathedral of the Church of Ireland. Built between 1220 and 1260, it stands on the site where it is believed St. Patrick baptized converts to

Christianity in the 5th century. The outside of St. Patrick's Cathedral is characterized by its pointed arches, intricate stonework, and soaring spire, which rises to a height of over 140 feet. Built from local limestone, the cathedral's exterior is imposing yet elegant, with large buttresses that support its towering walls. It was very gothic-looking. The western facade features a tall, ornate doorway framed by intricate carvings. Surrounding the cathedral are lush gardens, offering a serene contrast to the bustling city around it. These gardens are part of St. Patrick's Park, where you can find a statue of St. Patrick himself.

Inside, the cathedral was just as impressive. The vast nave is lined with rows of Gothic arches and high vaulted ceilings, giving the space an open and awe-inspiring feel. The sunlight filtering through the cathedral's stained-glass windows creates a warm, colorful glow that illuminates the intricate stonework and craftsmanship throughout the church. Many of these windows depict scenes from the life of St. Patrick, as well as other biblical stories and Irish history. Other key features include the medieval baptismal font and a collection of ancient manuscripts and historical artifacts displayed throughout the cathedral. I can tell you right now that we have absolutely nothing like this at all in the States, and it helps me to realize just how old Ireland really is. We spent about an hour and a half strolling around the cathedral, absorbing its grandeur and the profound sense of something far greater than ourselves. Each towering arch, intricate detail, and quiet corner seemed to whisper stories of faith, history, and human connection, leaving us both humbled and awestruck.

After leaving St. Patrick's Cathedral, we headed back into the lively streets of Dublin, making our way toward Trinity College. As we walked, we were met with an unexpected sight—a man fully dressed in Viking attire, complete with a fur cloak and helmet, leading a massive, wolf-like dog through the city. His costume was meticulously detailed, from the polished shield on his back to the intricate leather straps across his chest. The wolf-dog at his side added an air of authenticity, its striking appearance and calm demeanor making heads turn as they passed. The sight of this Viking and his beast amidst the modern cityscape created a captivating contrast, a reminder of Ireland's deep and storied history, blending seamlessly with the present-day vibrancy of Dublin.

The sight of that Viking was just so cool; it's hard to put into words. It was like stepping into another world for a moment—a fierce figure from Ireland's ancient past walking through the modern streets as if it were the most natural thing. The intensity of his Viking gear, the raw energy of that wolf-like dog by his side, and the surreal contrast of this historical warrior striding through Dublin felt like something straight out of a movie. It's the kind of experience that makes you feel a deep connection to the past, even if you're not sure how to describe it. Sometimes, words just don't capture the sheer awesomeness of a moment like that.

As we continued through the bustling streets of Dublin toward Trinity College, we couldn't help but admire the many charming shops and inviting restaurants along the way. Every street seemed to hold a unique energy, with locals and tourists blending seamlessly into the lively atmosphere. The crosswalks and stop signs were different from what we were used to in the U.S., but after a few crossings, we quickly figured them out.

What really caught my attention, though, were the buildings. Many were so old and filled with character that I found myself constantly looking up, taking in the intricate details, the weathered facades, and the history etched into every stone. It felt like the city itself was telling a story through its architecture.

Finally, we reached Trinity College—and the sight was breathtaking. The grandeur of the campus, with its iconic entrance and beautifully preserved buildings, left us in awe. It was as though we had stepped into a place where centuries of learning and history were still very much alive. The atmosphere was electric, and we couldn't wait to explore more of this legendary institution.

The grounds at Trinity College in Dublin are a blend of historical charm and vibrant green spaces. Established in 1592, the college features stunning architecture that reflects centuries of academic excellence. As you walk through the campus, you're greeted by beautifully manicured lawns, grand buildings, and cobblestone paths that echo with history. The grounds are spacious, with tall trees and open courtyards, offering a peaceful escape from the bustling city outside. Trinity College is also home to the iconic Long Room library and the Book of Kells.

We had pre-purchased tickets to visit the Long Room, a location I was especially excited about and high on my bucket list. Although they were in the process of refurbishing the iconic Long Room, where all the books are kept, it was still an incredible experience. The Long Room, with its high, arched ceilings and rows of ancient texts, houses around 200,000 of the library's oldest books. It is an awe-inspiring space, often described as one of the most beautiful libraries in the world. In the center of the room stands a large, illuminated world globe, adding to the grandeur.

We were also excited to see the Book of Kells. The Book of Kells is an illuminated manuscript that contains the four Gospels of the New Testament—Matthew, Mark, Luke, and John—written in Latin. It is one of the most important and beautifully crafted medieval artifacts, created by monks around 800 A.D. The manuscript is celebrated for its intricate artwork and detailed calligraphy, which combine Christian iconography with traditional Celtic designs.

The book's origin is traditionally associated with the monastery of Iona, off the coast of Scotland, but it was moved to Kells, Ireland, after Viking raids. Today, it resides at Trinity College Dublin, where it is on permanent display. The manuscript's pages are made from vellum[2], and each one is adorned with vibrant illustrations of religious figures, animals, and elaborate interwoven patterns.

I had hoped we would be able to view and turn the pages of some of the ancient books. Alas, we did not for obvious reasons, but we did get to see many of the intricate illustrations from the books on display. The level of detail in each drawing and every display was truly inspiring and humbling. It was a powerful reminder of the incredible craftsmanship and dedication that went into creating these works of art. So much time and effort had been dedicated to creating these works of art, and I couldn't help but wonder why we don't invest the same energy into creating art today. Seeing these beautifully hand-drawn books inspired me to use my time more wisely so I, too, could leave something meaningful behind, as these artists had. I left Trinity College feeling spiritually fulfilled with a renewed vision.

The next stop was the photo op locations we wanted to see. We walked a few blocks and found the Ha'Penny Bridge. The Ha'penny Bridge is one of Dublin's most iconic landmarks. Officially named the Liffey Bridge, it was built in 1816 and spans the River Liffey, connecting the areas of Temple Bar and the north side of the city. The bridge's distinctive white cast-iron arch design has made it one of the most photographed and recognizable structures in Dublin. I wanted to make sure everyone could see me standing at the River Liffey on the Ha'penny Bridge, so of course, I had to get a photo. Christina happily snapped the picture for me, capturing the moment perfectly.

The name "Ha'penny" comes from the half-penny toll that was originally charged to pedestrians who crossed it when it was first constructed. At the time, a ferry service operated by William Walsh was the primary way to cross the river, but with his ferry boats falling into disrepair, he was granted the right to build the bridge. In exchange, he was allowed to charge the toll, which remained in place for nearly 100 years before being abolished in 1919.

---

[2] calfskin

The Ha'penny Bridge is about 141 feet long and was the first pedestrian bridge over the River Liffey. Today, it is solely a pedestrian crossing, with thousands of people walking over it daily. Its charm lies not only in its history but also in its role as a key symbol of Dublin. Whether viewed during the day or illuminated at night, it offers a picturesque view of the river and the city, making it a favorite spot for tourists and one of our photo op sites.

We continued walking along the River Liffey until we found the Molly Malone statue, another photo op site on the list. The Molly Malone Statue is one of Dublin's most famous monuments, celebrating the city's rich folklore. Located on Suffolk Street near Trinity College, the statue depicts Molly Malone, a character from a popular Irish song titled "Cockles and Mussels." The song tells the story of a young woman who worked as a fishmonger, pushing her cart through the streets of Dublin, calling out, "Cockles and mussels, alive, alive-oh."

According to the ballad, Molly Malone was a beautiful fishmonger by day and, some versions suggest, a part-time street vendor. Tragically, she died young of a fever, and the song has immortalized her as an enduring symbol of the city.

The bronze statue, sculpted by Jeanne Rynhart, was unveiled in 1988 as part of Dublin's Millennium celebrations. It shows Molly standing beside her cart of shellfish, dressed in traditional 17th-century clothing with a low-cut blouse, which has made the statue a bit infamous for the way tourists rub her chest for good luck. Over time, this has become a quirky tradition for visitors, including us. Nothing wrong with rubbing a statue's boobs, right? Today, it remains a beloved attraction and a nod to Dublin's musical and cultural heritage, as well as its street vendors who have long been part of the city's history.

For reasons I can't fully explain, I already knew the song, *Molly Malone.* Its melody echoed in my mind, stirring questions about how it came to be a part of me. Was it because of my Irish ancestry? Did a relative once sing it to me, unknowingly planting its tune in my heart? I felt deeply humbled and profoundly happy to sense such an unexpected connection to this place—this land I had never set foot on before but somehow felt intertwined with my soul.

Angela wanted no part of rubbing Molly Malone's boobs, but Christina and I were all in—giggling like schoolgirls the entire time. We patiently waited our turn after the other tourists, and when our moment finally came, we stepped up to the statue and enthusiastically went to work, much to Angela's reluctant amusement as she snapped our photo. We couldn't stop laughing, partly from embarrassment and partly from the sheer ridiculousness of it all. The best part? Watching the mix of amusement and confusion on the faces of passersby as they watched us unabashedly rubbing Molly's infamous chest. It was awkward, hilarious, and oddly thrilling!

After the traditional boob rub of Molly Malone, we left in search of Temple Bar, a must-see while in Dublin. Temple Bar is one of Dublin's most famous and vibrant areas, known for its lively atmosphere, cobblestone streets, and rich cultural scene. We found the Temple Bar pub on the south bank of the River Liffey.

The Temple Bar pub—and the district itself—is not just a single bar but an entire area filled with pubs, restaurants, galleries, and cultural attractions.

The Temple Bar Pub, often referred to as the heart of the district, is one of the most iconic and visited spots in Dublin, and you can tell from all the tourists, including us. Established in 1840, the pub has a distinctive red exterior and is renowned for its traditional Irish music sessions, which attract both locals and tourists. And although the pub was extremely busy, it was a beautiful site! It looked just like the pictures from all my research. We did not enter the pub because it was too packed, but seeing the outside red exterior was more than enough, and hearing the lively music flowing out onto the cobbled streets was heartwarming.

By this time, we were starting to get hungry and worn out from all the walking. We decided to stop at one of the many restaurants, grab a bite to eat, and then head back to the hotel. Christina found a restaurant that was packed but definitely worth the wait. One of Christina's many talents was finding great places to eat. She'd proven herself many times over and did not disappoint when she found The Bank on College Green! The restaurant was absolutely stunning, with its grand architecture and historic charm adding to the experience.

The Bank on College Green is a well-known restaurant and bar located in the heart of Dublin, housed in a historic building that was once a bank. The building itself, originally constructed in 1892, is a stunning example of Victorian architecture, with grand ceilings, intricate woodwork, and stained-glass windows. It retains many of its original features, giving the space a luxurious and elegant atmosphere and making it one of the more unique dining venues in the city.

The restaurant offers a blend of traditional Irish and European dishes, all prepared with a focus on fresh, local ingredients. It is particularly popular for its seafood, steaks, and hearty Irish fare like Guinness stew and fresh oysters. The bar featured an extensive selection of wines, craft beers, and cocktails, as well as a solid range of Irish whiskeys, which allowed us to enjoy a full Irish dining experience.

What makes The Bank on College Green stand out is not only the food and drink but also the atmosphere. Dining here felt like stepping back in time, surrounded by the grandeur of Dublin's history. It was a unique blend of old-world charm and modern dining.

I opted for the Guinness Stew, which was hands down the best stew I've ever tasted—rich, flavorful, and perfectly cooked. Of course, no stew is complete without a side of the famous Irish brown bread, which was absolutely to die for. The combination was hearty and delicious, a true taste of Ireland.

Angela ordered the Shepard's Pie with peas and carrots. The shepherd's pie arrived steaming hot, its golden-brown topping crisp and flaky, with delicate layers that crumbled perfectly under the touch of a fork. Beneath the topping lay a hearty filling of savory ground meat, richly seasoned and simmered with onions, garlic, and a medley of herbs, all enveloped in a velvety gravy. Nestled alongside was a vibrant side of peas and carrots, their natural sweetness balanced with a touch of buttery warmth. The peas popped with freshness, while the tender carrots added a satisfying bite. I decided then that the next thing I was going to try was Shepard's Pie!

Christina asked our waitress to recommend the best dish on the menu, and she confidently replied that their most popular choice was the Seafood Chowder. So, Christina ordered the Seafood Chowder. We learned that at the Bank, homemade chowder is celebrated for its rich, creamy texture and generous portions of fresh seafood, including tender pieces of fish and clams, and those were valid claims! The flavors were perfectly balanced, delivering a satisfying depth without being overly fishy. Alongside the chowder, she was served a slice of traditional Irish soda bread.

Eager to try some traditional Irish drinks, we decided to make our first dining experience in Ireland truly memorable. At The Bank, we ordered a French Martini, a Negroni Bianco, and, naturally, a glass of Irish Whiskey. Each drink was expertly crafted and did not disappoint, highlighting the quality and care that went into their preparation. To fully embrace the experience, we shared bites from each other's plates and sipped each other's drinks, ensuring that no flavor or moment of this culinary adventure was missed.

I should also mention that I had made a list of Irish foods and drinks I wanted to try during my trip. By this point, I had happily crossed off a few items, but many more awaited me. My culinary adventure was far from over—there were still so many traditional dishes and drinks left to experience. From Fish and Chips to Irish Stew, I was determined to savor every bite of Irish culture through its food. Each meal felt like a deeper connection to my heritage, and I was committed to experiencing everything on my list before heading home, immersing myself fully in the flavors of Ireland.

After finishing our hearty meals, we decided to walk back to the hotel, taking the scenic route along the River Liffey. The evening air was cool, and the lights of Dublin reflected off the river's surface, casting a gentle glow on the cobbled streets. The rhythmic sound of our footsteps, combined with the faint music echoing from nearby pubs, created a peaceful contrast to the liveliness of the city. It felt as if Dublin itself was welcoming us, offering both its history and charm as we made our way back to the hotel. Each step along the river brought a deeper appreciation for this city, with its blend of modern life and rich tradition.

When we finally made it to the Harding Hotel, we were assigned a room on the third floor, which meant taking the lift[3]. The room was small but cozy, with three single beds—something I'd never seen in a hotel before, but it was absolutely perfect for the three of us.

The best part was the window, which offered a stunning view of Christ Church. It felt surreal to have such a historic landmark right outside our window. After dropping off our backpacks, Christina and I decided to head next door to Darkey Kelly's for an authentic Irish pub experience. Meanwhile, Angela, ever the adventurer, rented a bike and set off to explore more of the city on her own.

With excitement bubbling inside us, we rode the lift back down to the lobby and made our way down two flights of stairs to Darkey Kelly's. The moment we opened the door, we were immersed in the most authentic Irish experience I'd ever encountered. The sound of traditional Irish music filled the air, mingling with the hum of lively conversations in rich Irish accents. The energy was electric, and the pub was packed with locals, creating the perfect atmosphere.

As soon as we entered, a friendly waitress spotted us and quickly escorted us to a table, asking for our drink orders with a warm smile. She guessed right away that we were Americans, and when we confirmed, she grinned and said, "You're going to start with a Guinness, and after that, you'll try the red beer." Christina and I exchanged excited glances and happily agreed with a laugh, "Okay!"

For Christina and me, this was the quintessential Irish experience we had been dreaming of. Everything about it felt alive and real—the music, the people, and the culture—and we couldn't have been happier to be part of it.

From the moment we stepped inside Darkey Kelly's, the atmosphere hit us like a wave of warmth and energy. The pub was packed, with people seated at every table, and the wooden floors echoed with the lively shuffle of feet. In the corner, a small stage hosted a group of musicians playing traditional Irish instruments, their upbeat tunes filling the room with an irresistible rhythm.

As they played, the crowd erupted into song, joining in with a traditional Irish tune. I didn't know the song, but that didn't matter—the sheer joy in the room was contagious. Soon, people were stomping their feet on the wooden floor in time with the music, adding to the rhythm and energy of the moment. The sound of stomping feet reverberated through the pub, blending with the clinking of glasses and laughter, making it feel like the floor was alive with the spirit of the gathering.

---

[3] Elevator

It was like a scene out of a movie, something I'd only ever seen on TV. Yet here I was, experiencing it firsthand—the music, the singing, the stomping feet, and the sheer happiness of everyone around me. It felt magical, and I was thrilled to be part of such an authentic, unforgettable moment.

The Guinness was unlike anything I'd ever tasted back in the U.S.—it was rich, smooth, and so fresh it felt like a completely different drink. We quickly chugged them down, savoring every drop. Next up was Smithwick's Irish Red Ale, the second most popular beer in Ireland. Lighter than the Guinness but just as delicious, we knocked back a couple more glasses, all while chatting with the friendly patrons who passed by our table.

Many stopped to strike up conversations with "the Americans," curious about where we were from. When we mentioned Texas, their eyes lit up, and they couldn't resist poking fun at our accents. It was all in good humor, and their excitement was infectious. It was wonderful to sit there, meeting so many people, with everyone asking if we were there for work or "on holiday," as they called it, which sounded so cool to hear in that context.

These wonderfully enchanting people were nothing like those haters on social media. In fact, I had yet to meet anyone who wasn't helpful and friendly.

Just then, the band launched into Bon Jovi's *Livin' on a Prayer,* and Christina and I, buzzing from all the beer, jumped right in, singing at the top of our lungs. It was an incredible moment—two Texans in an Irish pub, belting out an American classic, surrounded by the warmth and laughter of the crowd. It felt like pure joy, an unforgettable night where everything just fell perfectly into place.

Eventually, it was time to call it a night, even though none of us really wanted to leave. We would have stayed until closing if we didn't have plans for the next day. As we reluctantly left the pub, I realized this had been one of the happiest days of my life, and for two reasons.

First, I was in Ireland, in a true Irish pub, having the time of my life—feeling more alive and connected than ever before. Second, when we made it back to our room and settled in for the night, I received a notification that made my heart soar.

My name had appeared on a Google website. Curious and excited, I quickly researched why and discovered that it was linked to my new book. There it was—my name, *Mica Boyd Johnston*, followed by the word "Author." At that moment, I was overwhelmed with pride and humility. To be living one of my greatest dreams in Ireland and, at the same time, seeing my name officially recognized as an author was beyond anything I could have imagined. There are no words to fully describe how grateful I felt right then. It was a moment of fulfilled happiness and deep contentment, one that I will associate with the Magic of Ireland.

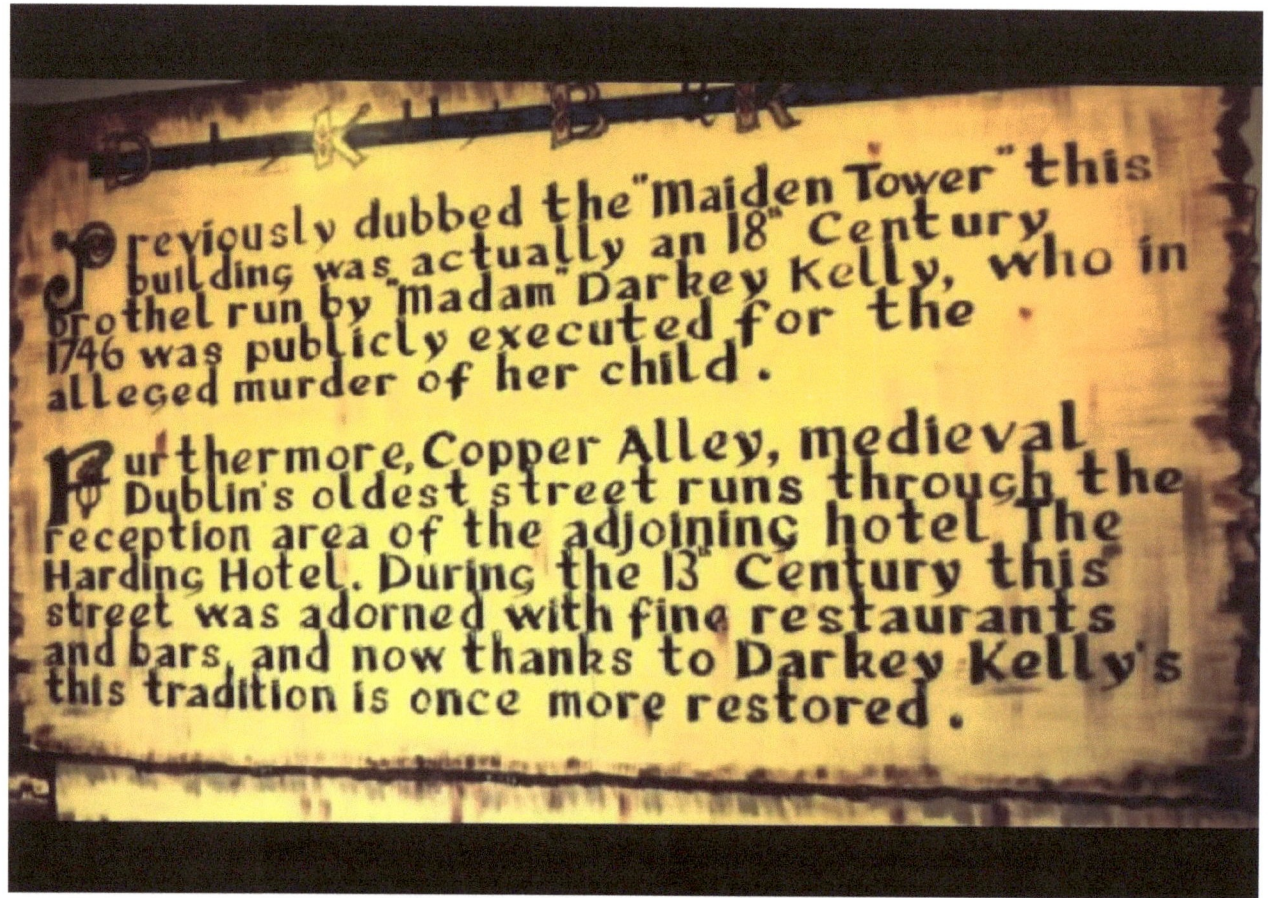

Previously dubbed the "Maiden Tower" this building was actually an 18th Century brothel run by "madam" Darkey Kelly, who in 1746 was publicly executed for the alleged murder of her child.

Furthermore, Copper Alley, medieval Dublin's oldest street runs through the reception area of the adjoining hotel, The Harding Hotel. During the 13th Century this street was adorned with fine restaurants and bars, and now thanks to Darkey Kelly's this tradition is once more restored.

CHAPTER FOUR: VIKINGS

Day 2:

Day 2 kicked off wonderfully! We all woke up early and headed down the lift to the hotel's restaurant. Isn't it fascinating how quickly we adapt to the language and accents of another country when we travel? For example, during our time in Ireland, we stopped saying "elevator" and started calling it "the lift," just like the locals. This is one of the most interesting aspects of traveling — how we become immersed in the culture. By adopting local words, expressions, and ways of speaking, we gain a deeper understanding of the people, their habits, and their values. Cultural exchanges like these enrich our experiences and offer valuable insights into the diversity of the world around us. It was only our second day, yet we were already beginning to feel like the locals. We were experiencing their way of life, picking up their habits, and even adopting their language. It's amazing how quickly you can become immersed in a new culture, almost as if you've always belonged there.

The hotel's restaurant, The Copper Alley Bistro, is tucked away within the Harding Hotel, adding to its cozy and intimate charm. To reach it, we walked through the hotel lobby and up a gentle incline to a long hallway and then a narrow doorway that invited us inside. The bistro's stained-glass windows were a highlight, depicting vibrant scenes of a Viking ship sailing across the ocean. The intricate designs and rich glass colors added a touch of history and artistry, setting the tone for a warm and welcoming dining experience. Our waitress sat us next to large bay windows overlooking the streets of Dublin. From our spot, we were able to watch the city slowly wake up and come to life.

Christina and I ordered the traditional Irish breakfast of eggs, bacon, hashbrowns, and toast, while Angela opted for the waffles. We savored our delicious breakfast at a leisurely pace, taking in the serene morning atmosphere while watching early risers stroll along the cobblestone streets outside. The quiet hum of the city waking up mirrored our growing excitement for the day ahead. As the anticipation bubbled within us, we finished our meal, drank the last of our coffee, and stepped outside, ready to embrace the next adventure awaiting us.

We left the Harding Hotel and didn't have far to go for our 10 a.m. excursion at the Viking Museum, also known as Dublinia. Fun fact: the name "Dublin" originates from the Scandinavian word for "black pool." The name "Black Pool" comes from the Old Norse name "Dubh Linn." The Vikings, who settled in Dublin around the 9th century, gave the city this name. "Dubh" means "black" in Old Norse, and "Linn" refers to a pool or a pond. The name "Dubh Linn" was likely inspired by a dark tidal pool or lagoon that existed near where the River Liffey meets the sea, which the Vikings used as a docking area for their ships. Over time, "Dubh Linn" evolved into the modern name, Dublin. I had no idea just how deeply Dublin is rooted in Viking history. While doing research, I came across information about the Viking Museum, but I had no idea how rich and extensive the Viking influence in the city really was. Learning about this fascinating history brought me so much joy and gave me a whole new perspective on Dublin.

I was buzzing with excitement, eager to immerse myself in the rich history of the Vikings! When I came across Dublinia, I was determined to visit. I initially tried to book tickets in advance, but to my disappointment, they were sold out. Still, I didn't give up hope. The day before we left, I checked again, hoping for a cancellation—and I got lucky! I managed to secure tickets for Sunday, May 19th. Although it meant rearranging a few parts of my original itinerary, it was absolutely worth it. One valuable lesson I learned from this experience is that plans can always be adjusted, and sometimes, a little persistence pays off.

By the time we arrived at Dublinia, a line was already forming. I was practically bouncing with anticipation! My heart was racing, and I couldn't stop myself from chattering nervously—I was so thrilled to be there finally! The energy was electric, and I felt like a kid on Christmas morning, ready to dive into the world of Vikings!

The Dublinia Museum was an absolute thrill from start to finish! One of the first things we did was write our names in Viking runes—how cool is that?! Then, we got to try on authentic-looking Viking helmets and even had a sword fight! It was like stepping straight into history. We also tried on traditional Viking garb, which made us feel like we were part of the ancient Norse world.

Everywhere we looked, there were fascinating historical displays and real artifacts from the Viking era—actual treasures of the past right in front of us! They even told us that across the street, Viking bones had been uncovered from multiple burials, which added a whole new layer of awe to the experience.

The Dublinia Museum building itself is like a journey through time! It's a striking, medieval-style structure that instantly immerses you in the atmosphere of ancient Dublin. The exterior is made of stone, with towering walls that give it an imposing, fortress-like feel. Inside, the building is wonderfully old, with narrow passageways and creaky wooden floors that seem to whisper of history.

It's a bit cold and drafty, which only adds to the authenticity, making you feel as if you've stepped back in time. The high, arched ceilings and stone walls create an air of mystery, with dim lighting that cast shadows across the historical exhibits. There's a steeple at the top, where the open windows let in streams of light, offering a breathtaking view over the city of Dublin. The entire structure feels rugged and ancient, the perfect home for a museum dedicated to the Viking era. It's almost as if the building itself is a relic from the past! Walking up to the steeple to gaze out over Dublin was an unforgettable experience. As we climbed the winding staircase, the anticipation grew with every step. Once at the top, the view took our breath away. The city stretched out beneath us, its mix of historic buildings, winding streets, and modern life blending together in a beautiful tapestry. From this vantage point, Dublin seemed both timeless and alive, with the River Liffey cutting through the heart of the city and the distant hills providing a stunning backdrop. It was a moment that allowed me to truly appreciate the city's charm and its rich history from a whole new perspective.

We descended the staircase, and it led us through what felt like an ancient medieval church. The long stone hallway, lined with beautiful stained-glass windows, made it seem like we had stumbled into a hidden part of the building. For a moment, I was convinced we had taken a wrong turn and ended up somewhere off-limits!

After many steps down the long hallway, we reached two young men standing in front of massive wooden doors, easily 8 feet tall. Without a word, they silently opened the doors, and in an instant, bright sunlight flooded in, accompanied by the loud, vibrant sounds of the city. We were back on the bustling streets of Dublin, the quiet of the hallway replaced by the energy of the city in a heartbeat. Just like that, our incredible Viking Museum adventure had come to an end. It was such a mind-blowing experience, one I know I'll never forget!

If you ever have the chance to visit Dublin, be sure to check out the Dublinia Museum to explore the city's rich Viking history. The Vikings established a strong presence in Dublin over a thousand years ago, leaving a lasting impact on the city's culture and development. Dublinia offers an immersive experience where you can walk through Viking-era streets, see reconstructed Viking houses, and learn about the daily life, trade, and battles of these fascinating seafaring people. It's a must-visit for anyone interested in understanding how the Vikings shaped Dublin into the vibrant city it is today.

Once outside on the lively streets of Dublin, we made our way to a bus stop and decided to hop on the famous hop-on-hop-off bus while waiting for our next tour. It's such a fun way to explore the city, riding through the streets while soaking in all the important landmarks and incredible views.

The hop-on-hop-off buses in Dublin are an incredibly popular and convenient way to explore the city, especially for first-time visitors like us. These double-decker buses follow carefully curated routes that take you to all of Dublin's must-see landmarks and attractions, offering a flexible and enjoyable way to sightsee. You can hop off at any stop that catches your interest, spend as much time as you'd like exploring, and then simply hop back on when you're ready to continue your adventure.

Some of the sights we saw were as follows:

- **Trinity College**: We drove around the college and saw how very large it really is.
- **Guinness Storehouse**: Our next tour for the day, so that was cool to see beforehand.
- **Dublin Castle**: A real castle that dates back to the 13th century.
- **St. Patrick's Cathedral**: We had already visited, but it was breathtaking to see it again.
- **Temple Bar**: We drove around the many streets in the Temple Bar area.
- **Kilmainham Gaol**: A former prison that looked kind of like a museum.
- **Teeling Whiskey Museum**: Very cool site and very interesting!
- **Old Jameson Distillery**: A very cool old and imposing building!
- **Pearse Lyons Distillery**: I'm starting to see a theme!
- **Phoenix Park**: We hopped off here for a photo op. It was beautiful!
- **Heuston Station**: The massive train station in Dublin.

Our bus came equipped with our very own live guide and his beautiful Irish accent, delivering audio commentary. We learned fascinating stories and history about each stop and the city's heritage, too. Our guide was charming and witty and had that signature Irish humor! I wish I could remember his name. I made it a point to write down everyone's name that we were fortunate to interact with going forward. I wanted to remember everything about this wonderful country and its people.

We hopped off the bus at Phoenix Park, eager to explore its expansive beauty. Spanning over 1,700 acres, it's one of the largest enclosed parks in Europe, home to vast green meadows, wooded areas, and historic landmarks. As we walked through the park, we came across the towering Wellington Monument, an impressive obelisk that stands 62 meters tall (about 204 feet for my fellow Americans), dedicated to the Duke of Wellington, who famously defeated Napoleon at the Battle of Waterloo. The sun was shining brightly, with no clouds in the sky, and the park was alive, with people enjoying the warm weather. Sunbathers were scattered across the grassy fields, basking in the rare Irish sunshine, creating a lively yet peaceful atmosphere.

With excitement, we climbed the stairs of the Wellington Monument, each step rewarding us with breathtaking views of Phoenix Park! Reaching the top felt like a triumph, and the panoramic scene below made it all worthwhile. But going back down? That was a whole other story—it was brutal on my knees! By the time we reached the bottom, my knees were practically screaming for mercy. Thankfully, we decided to hop on another bus and head to the Guinness Brewery—just in time! My legs definitely needed a break after that climb, but what an incredible experience it was!

When we first boarded the second bus, we asked the young man driving the bus, Ian (I wrote down his name this time), about the fare. With a delightful Irish accent, he replied, "Tree pounds." I couldn't resist playfully mimicking his accent, saying, "Tree pounds?" He smiled and explained that's how they say "three" in Ireland. A little later, he reminded all the passengers, over the intercom, why the Irish don't pronounce the "h" sound, and I immediately felt terrible, worried I might have unintentionally hurt his feelings.

Ian told us that The Irish pronunciation of "three" as "tree" is a characteristic of the Irish English accent, influenced by the phonetics of the Irish language (Gaeilge) and certain historical linguistic patterns. In Irish (Gaeilge), there is no "th" sound like in English. Instead, the Irish use sounds that more closely resemble "t" or "d." When Irish speakers learned English historically, they often carried over these pronunciations. It's a fascinating example of how accents and speech patterns develop from historical and cultural contexts.

When we got off the bus, I made sure to tip generously and told him my remark was made with nothing but good intentions. I also let him know how much I love the Irish and their charming accent. His smile reassured me, and I left feeling happy and grateful for such a wonderful experience and to learn something more about these wonderful people.

After riding the hop-on-hop-off bus and walking through Phoenix Park, we definitely started to feel hungry. We walked around the streets by the Guinness Brewery and stumbled upon the most charming three-story Bistro. A place called Harkin's Bar & Bistro. It was the perfect spot to grab a cold Guinness and maybe check off another item from my food list!

Waiting at the front door was a delightful Irish man, and when I asked his name, I could not understand what he said. He was smoking a cigarette and looked quite content. He asked if we were ready for a pint, to which we assured him we were, and he smiled a huge smile showing a mouthful of teeth, and in the thickest Irish accent I had heard yet, he said, *"Yerr in de rroight place!"* He opened the door and motioned us in, and when we entered, it was just as you would have imagined a traditional Irish pub to look like.

Upon entering the first floor, we noticed the wooden flooring with small tables and stools scattered around a fully stocked bar. The space was small, with about a dozen or so seats, all of which were occupied. A friendly young woman greeted us and suggested heading to the next floor, assuring us there were plenty of available seats upstairs.

We climbed a narrow, cozy stairwell to the second floor, where we found ourselves a table. The second floor was a bit more modern, with stylish black leather seats and tables. Not long after sitting, another cheerful waitress came by to take our order. We all ordered a pint of Guinness, and let me tell you—the Guinness arrived in record time! I swear, they must have had glasses pre-poured because it showed up almost instantly. I couldn't help but laugh, thinking they probably knew everyone wanted a pint of Guinness.

Just as I was enjoying my drink, nature called. I had been savoring the smooth richness of my pint, letting the cozy hum of conversation and the faint strains of traditional Irish music wrap around me like a warm blanket. But when nature calls, you answer—especially after a pint or two.

I caught the attention of our waitress, Saoirse [4](at least, I *think* that's how her name was pronounced—I was still getting the hang of Irish names, which seemed to dance off the tongue with a rhythm all their own). Her smile was bright, and she leaned in slightly over the table to hear me better over the buzz of the crowded pub.

"Where's the restroom?" I asked.

---

[4] Pronounced sear + sha means freedom and liberty.

For a split second, her expression faltered. It was subtle, but I caught it—a slight furrow of her brow, a flicker of hesitation. Then, her smile returned as she gestured toward a narrow, dimly lit stairwell tucked away in the corner.

"Down the stairs, love. Just head down to the basement. You'll find it there," she said with that unmistakable Irish lilt.

I thanked her, but as I stood up, I couldn't help but smirk to myself. That tiny pause, that flash of confusion—it reminded me of my first night in Ireland at *Darkey Kelly's.* I'd had the same interaction with a bartender, except his reaction was far less subtle. I had walked up to the bar and asked for the "bathroom," and he froze, beer tap in hand, staring at me like I'd just asked where the spaceship was parked.

"Uh… the *what*?" he asked, eyebrows knitting together.

"The bathroom?" I repeated hesitantly.

It wasn't until another patron leaned over and said, "She means the *toilet*, mate," that the bartender nodded, pointed toward a hallway, and sent me on my way. I had been so flustered that I practically speed-walked to the facilities, cheeks flushed.

Apparently, "bathroom" isn't the go-to term in Ireland. They say *toilet* or sometimes *loo*. And while they'll generally understand "bathroom," "restroom" seems to be the real head-scratcher—it's as if the term doesn't quite compute. I couldn't blame them, though. If you think about it, the word *restroom* does sound oddly euphemistic. Who goes there to *rest* anyway?

Back in the present moment, I carefully made my way down the creaky staircase Saoirse had pointed out. The air in the basement was noticeably cooler, and the old stone walls gave the space a slightly medieval vibe, as though I'd stumbled into a secret dungeon pub. The restroom was tucked at the end of a narrow hallway, marked with a simple sign—*Toilet.* No frills, no confusion.

As I washed my hands and prepared to head back upstairs, I caught my reflection in the mirror and laughed softly to myself. These little cultural hiccups, these brief moments of being slightly out of sync with the rhythm of a new place—they were part of the charm of travel. Sure, asking for the restroom might not have been my smoothest moment, but it was a lesson learned.

When I returned to the table, Saoirse gave me a quick nod and an amused smile, as if she somehow knew I'd been replaying that interaction in my head. I lifted my pint in her direction, silently toasting her patience and the subtle art of cross-cultural communication—one awkward question at a time.

All these stairs in Ireland! Between the multi-level buildings and all the walking, it's no wonder everyone here seems to be in such great shape. Meanwhile, after just a quick bathroom trip, I felt totally out of breath and needed a minute to recover!

We had a few minutes to relax before our next tour, so we ordered another Guinness and some food. While waiting for the food, we admired the many pictures lining the walls of the bistro. Most were nostalgic photos of old patrons and historic places, adding to the place's charm. Outside, the patio was packed with hungry and thirsty travelers, but despite their tired expressions, everyone seemed happy, soaking up the good vibes. I love that everyone seemed so cheerful everywhere we went!

I ordered a hamburger with fries. It was one of the thickest hamburgers I had ever seen. A thick piece of meat with two large buns, lettuce, tomato, and their own secret sauce. The burger looked absolutely mouthwatering. The fries came in a cute little metal cup overflowing. The fries were crispy on the outside and soft and tender on the inside.

I can't stand how quickly time slips away when you're enjoying yourself with friends in such a warm and inviting atmosphere, and just like that, it was time for our tour to start! Our tickets for the Guinness Brewery tour were at 3 PM, so we needed to head over. Luckily, it was just a short walk from Harkins to the brewery entrance. When we arrived, there was already a long line for the tour, but it moved quickly. The door crew efficiently scanned tickets, and before we knew it, we were welcomed inside for the experience!

Now, I'll admit—I didn't know much about Guinness other than it's a legendary beer in Ireland and something of a national treasure. It's not the type of beer I would typically drink back in the States, where my one and only experience with it left me unimpressed. But when I started planning this trip, the idea of visiting a real Irish brewery, especially one as iconic as Guinness, felt like a must-do. Anything that embodied the essence of Ireland seemed worth experiencing. So, without hesitation, one of the first things I did was book tickets for a tour of the Guinness Brewery.

Despite not being much of a beer drinker, I was genuinely excited about this tour. I'd read over and over in my research that Guinness in Ireland is a completely different experience—richer, fresher, and so much better than anywhere else. There was this air of mystery and promise about tasting it right at the source, where the tradition of brewing it runs so deep. Even though I hadn't fallen in love with it back home, I was eager to give it another try here in Dublin, where the beer's heart and soul are truly felt. I could already imagine the smooth, creamy pint in my hand as I soaked in the Irish atmosphere, ready to discover what all the fuss was about.

As soon as we stepped into the foyer of the Guinness Brewery, we were absolutely blown away by the sheer scale of the place. It was massive, almost overwhelming in its grandeur. Right in the center of the foyer, there was a breathtaking open space that stretched all the way up to the seventh floor, where we could glimpse the famous rooftop bar. The entire space was a marvel of industrial beauty—each floor represented a different stage of the brewing process, and everywhere we looked, there were gleaming pipes, intricate tubes, and towering stills. It was a real, working brewery in every sense, and you could feel that from the moment you walked in.

The air was alive with the hum of activity. The buzz of visitors echoed off the steel and glass, filling the space with energy. You could hear the clanging of machinery and the murmur of excited voices as people soaked in the surroundings. Our tour guide began explaining what we were about to experience, but even her voice echoed in this cavernous space, adding to the sense of wonder. It was as if every sound bounced off the walls, making the whole place feel even more vibrant and alive. The combination of sights, sounds, and the sheer magnitude of the brewery made it feel like we were stepping into the very heart of Guinness' legacy—a living, breathing monument to centuries of craftsmanship.

As we made our way through the first floor of the Guinness Brewery, we were instantly captivated by the whole experience. The walls were alive with state-of-the-art electric displays, vividly explaining each step of the brewing process. It felt like we were part of something cutting-edge yet deeply rooted in tradition. Then, we stumbled upon one of the most impressive sights—a waterfall that periodically spelled out "Guinness" in the cascading water. It was truly a breathtaking piece of artistry, blending nature and technology in the most magical way.

We learned that Guinness is made from just four ingredients—water, barley, hops, and yeast—but the fascinating part was that these ingredients have been sourced from the same families and places for generations. That kind of legacy and commitment to tradition was awe-inspiring. As we toured each floor, discovering the rich history of Guinness and Ireland, I couldn't shake the feeling that I had missed out on so much of this heritage. It made me wonder—what other pieces of history had I overlooked?

We continued walking and chatting, soaking in the knowledge on each floor. On one floor, we had the chance to taste Guinness in small glasses. I took a sip, and to my surprise, it was incredible—the smoothest, richest beer I'd ever had. It was worlds apart from my previous experience back home.

At last, we reached the seventh floor, where we ordered a pint of Guinness with a unique twist—the foam head had our pictures printed into it! It was a fun, personal touch that made the moment even more special. We took our beers and found a spot by a large bay window that offered a panoramic view of Dublin. Sitting there, sipping the freshest Guinness while overlooking the city, felt absolutely magical. It was a moment of pure contentment, where history, culture, and experience all came together in the most unforgettable way.

Once we finished our pints, we took the lift back down to the lobby, where we stumbled upon the gift shop. I couldn't resist—I had to get a Guinness souvenir! In fact, I went a bit overboard and bought gifts for everyone I knew. It might have been a little silly since they hadn't experienced Guinness the way I had, but I figured I could at least try to share the magic of the brewery with them through these mementos. Maybe, just maybe, I could convey the awe and excitement I felt while handing out the gifts.

With our bags full of souvenirs, we stepped back out onto the lively streets of Dublin, ready to track down a taxi to take us back to the hotel. I was feeling a little buzzed, incredibly happy, and full of energy. The whole experience had been so amazing, and I was already looking forward to another fun night at Darkey Kelly's—singing, stomping, and soaking in that pure Irish joy.

We found a taxi and took a short ride back to what would be our last night at the Harding Hotel. I already knew I was going to miss this place, especially Darkey Kelly's. Determined to make our final night unforgettable, I was ready to enjoy every moment before we left the next morning. We arrived at the hotel with hearts full of happiness and bellies full of beer. After dropping off our bags of souvenirs and freshening up, we were eager to head back to Darkey Kelly's for one last night of fun.

We had an early tour scheduled the next day, but at that moment, we didn't care at all. The plan was simple: embrace the full traditional Irish pub experience, even if it meant feeling rough in the morning. After freshening up, Christina and I made our way down to Darkey Kelly's while Angela decided to rent another bike and explore the city one last time.

We couldn't resist entering the pub through the secret entrance this time, something we had giggled about in the room. It felt so silly, but it added a layer of excitement that I can't help but smile about now. We ventured down another flight of stairs, pressed a hidden button, and watched as an invisible doorway swung open, leading us inside from the opposite side we had entered the night before. It was such a small thing, but it made us feel like we were on an adventure.

Once inside, the atmosphere was just as lively as before. The same waitress from the night before spotted us and waved us over, motioning for us to sit closer to the small stage. The music was already playing, and people were having a grand time. I knew right then that this night would be the perfect way to cap off our time at the Harding—full of laughter, music, and the magic of Ireland.

I have to tell you about something we discovered almost immediately on our second night at Darkey Kelly's. The waitress, who must have been a manager or just incredibly attentive, seemed determined to ensure everyone had a seat. When she sat us at our small table, there was an extra chair left open. Not long after, she motioned for a man to sit with us. At first, I found it a bit odd to share our table with a stranger, but we quickly realized this was standard practice in Irish pubs—no seat goes unused.

Our waitress explained, "Every seat is fair game." True to her word, I watched her pull barrels from behind the bar and place them strategically for those without seats. As more people arrived, she would guide them to the next available spot with a simple "Sit here." It was fascinating to see how seamlessly the pub accommodated everyone, creating a welcoming and communal atmosphere.

For anyone visiting Ireland, here's an interesting tidbit: in Irish pubs, they don't mess around when it comes to making space. Empty seats simply don't exist!

The gentleman who joined us was incredibly charming, with the thickest and most delightful Irish accent. His name was Martin, and as we chatted, we found out he was married to an American woman and lived in Kansas City, Missouri. He had traveled back home to Ireland to visit family and decided to spend the evening at the pub. We were more than happy to share our table and immerse ourselves in the Irish pub way.

We spent hours talking, laughing, and singing along to the music with Martin, who had such a warm, friendly energy. It felt like we'd known him for years. When we mentioned we had to cut the night short because of an early tour the next morning, Martin shared a piece of advice I'll never forget. He looked at us with a twinkle in his eye and said, "Enjoy every minute of your life because you'll be a long time dead."

Well, Christina and I could not argue with that logic, so we decided to stay a bit longer, singing, drinking, and enjoying the moment until we finally stumbled to the lift and back to our room, giggling all the way. It was one of those perfect nights that I'll hold dear forever.

GUINNESS

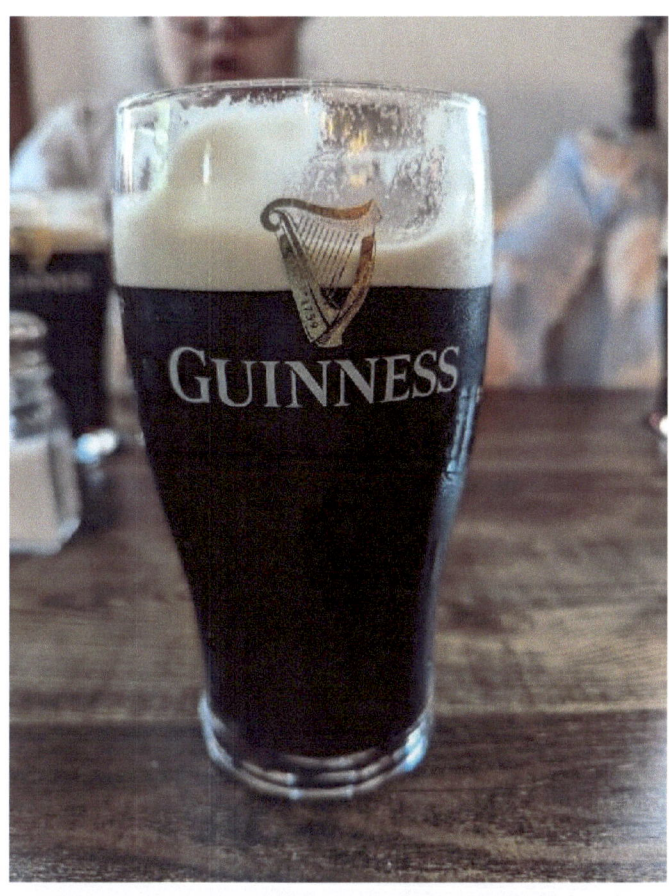

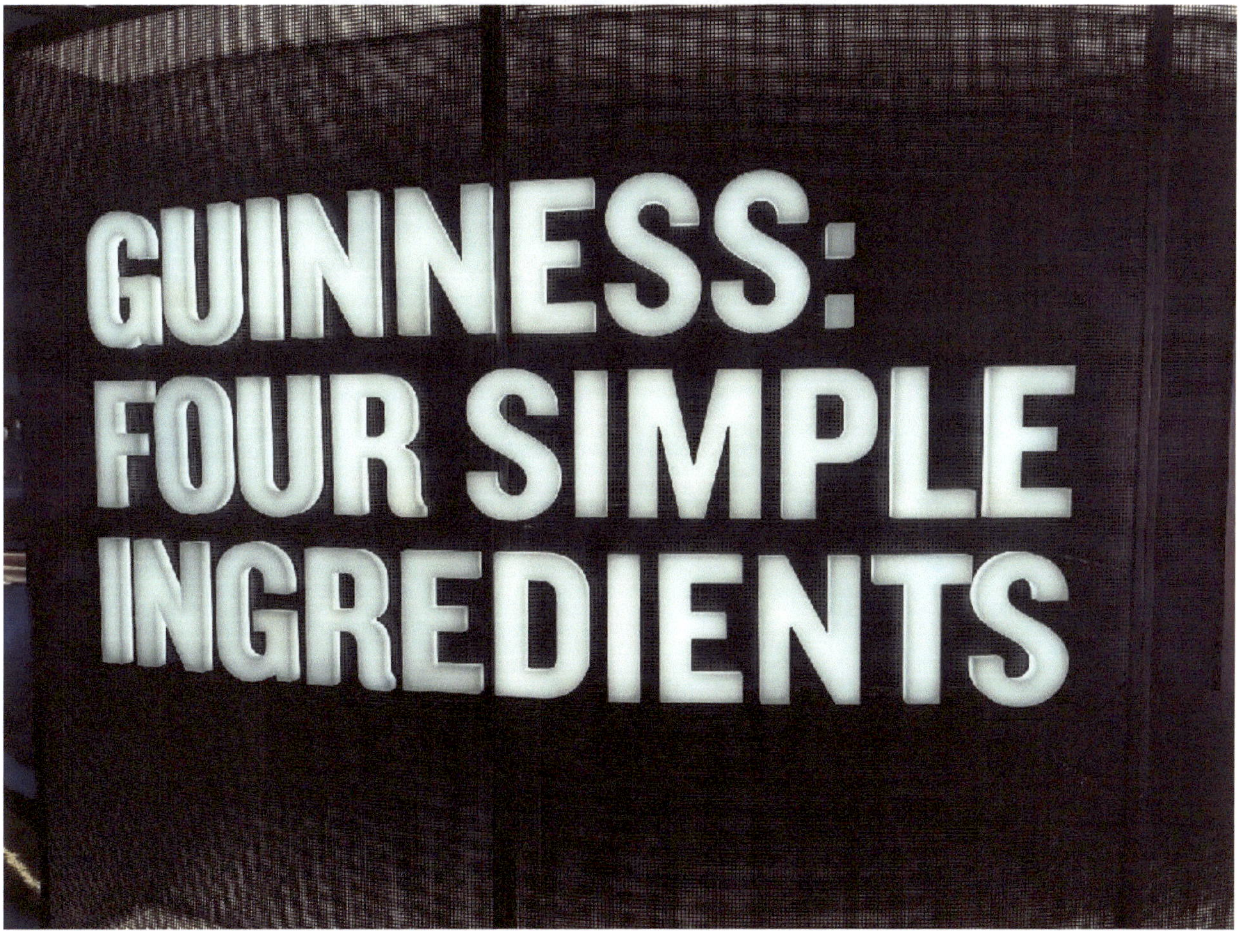
GUINNESS:
FOUR SIMPLE
INGREDIENTS

CHAPTER FIVE: NEWGRANGE

Day 3:

We all woke up surprisingly early the next morning, feeling refreshed despite the lively night before. I headed down the lift, eagerly anticipating a strong cup of coffee, though I was pleasantly surprised to find I didn't have the hangover I had expected—maybe that's part of the magic of Guinness. As we walked through the familiar corridor, taking the narrow passageway into the small restaurant, I felt a sense of calm and happiness. It was as if the Harding Hotel had become a home away from home. A familiar place that felt comfortable and safe.

Once again, breakfast was a delight, made even more special by the warm and friendly waitstaff who had welcomed us so graciously the day before. Angela, Christina, and I lingered at the table, chatting excitedly about our adventures from the previous day. There's something magical about traveling—the way it sparks meaningful conversations and brings people closer. Sharing experiences, laughter, and joy with those by your side creates bonds that feel deeper and more lasting with every moment.

After our meal, we packed up our things and said our goodbyes to the staff at the Harding. I knew right then that I would stay there again without a doubt—it had left such a warm imprint on my heart.

With our backpacks slung over our shoulders, we set off on the walk to Ned Kelly's, the meeting point for our all-day tour to Newgrange. The walk was a bit longer than I had anticipated, and my legs ached by the time we arrived, but the journey through the streets of Dublin was still enjoyable. You know the saying, "It's a good hurt."

At the meeting point for our tour bus to Newgrange, we struck up conversations with some of the other travelers. Many were visiting Ireland for the first time, and most were from America. Hearing their stories and shared excitement made me smile—it was heartwarming to realize how many Americans feel a deep connection to Ireland, just as I do.

During my research on Ireland, I read about a portal in Dublin that connected people in Dublin with those in New York City. Luckily for us, Angela brought to our attention that the portal was around the corner from where we were waiting on our tour bus. Excitedly. We walked over to the portal, and as we gazed into it, we were transported across the Atlantic, watching in real-time how people in New York City bustled through their day. The contrast was striking: the rhythm of Dublin around us blended with the energy of Manhattan visible through the portal. It was surreal to stand there, rooted in one city, yet feel so connected to another halfway across the world. The moment reminded us of how small and interconnected the world truly is.

Before long, the tour bus arrived, maneuvering through Dublin's now-congested streets. We climbed aboard, settling in for the hour-long journey to Newgrange. As the bus rumbled away from the city, I felt a peaceful sense of contentment, ready to experience the ancient history of Ireland but carrying with me the comfort and joy of the last couple of days, like I had found a new home in Dublin.

The ride to Newgrange was incredibly comfortable, and the scenery was nothing short of spectacular. As we traveled through the rolling Irish countryside, we were surrounded by vast, lush green fields stretching as far as the eye could see, dotted with sheep and stone fences that gave the landscape a timeless quality. Along the way, I noticed many road signs written in both Gaelic and English, with the Gaelic text in bold, larger letters above the smaller English translations. We learned that children in Ireland are now being taught Gaelic alongside English in school, which I thought was such a beautiful way to preserve their heritage and language.

The hour-long ride passed quickly, and before we knew it, we arrived at our first stop: Knowth. From the moment we stepped off the bus, it was clear that Knowth was something truly special. The site is home to some of the most significant and well-preserved ancient burial mounds in Ireland, even older than the pyramids of Egypt. The largest mound, encircled by smaller satellite tombs, immediately caught our attention. It was massive and mysterious, its grassy slopes blending into the landscape, but the real wonder lay in the intricately carved stones that lined the base of the mound. These stones were covered in ancient spirals, swirls, and geometric patterns that have withstood the test of time—symbols that no one fully understands but that feel connected to something deep and ancient.

Walking around the site, we learned from our Guide, Debra, that Knowth had been used by many different people over the millennia, evolving from a Neolithic burial site to a place of importance during the Iron Age. The sense of history was almost overwhelming as if the stones themselves were whispering stories of those who had come long before us. The quiet beauty and deep significance of Knowth made it feel like we were stepping back in time, and it left a lasting impression on all of us. It was more than just a stop on a tour—it was a journey into Ireland's ancient soul.

According to our guidebook:

Knowth is the largest of the three great monuments of the Brú na Bóinne complex in the Bend of the Boyne and the largest Neolithic passage tomb on the island of Ireland. It was built around 3300 BCE. There are 18 smaller satellite mounds around it, and the great monument itself originally had 127 curb stones, of which 124 survived. Knowth's maximum diameter is around 96 meters (approximately 315 feet). Knowth has two passages. The passages open towards the east and west and extend almost all the way into the center of the mound. The eastern passage is the longest of any Irish passage tomb and, at 40m (approximately 131 feet) long, the longest in western Europe. Knowth contains a magnificent array of megalithic art – more than any other Neolithic monument in Western Europe. Ninety of its 124 curb stones are decorated, and many stones in its passages/chambers are also heavily decorated. In mythology, Knowth is named in honor of two goddesses – Buí and Englec – according to the Dindshenchas (Lore of Places). Some of the megalithic art at Knowth appears to depict calendrical calculations, particularly relating to an attempt to correlate the lunar year with the solar year. In early medieval times, it became the capital of the kingdom of Northern Brega.

I might also add that the *Dindshenchas* (pronounced "din-HEN-chas") is the Irish lore preserved in poetry and early storytelling. Medieval manuscripts like *The Book of Leinster* and *The Book of Ballymote* recount the history and mythology of gods, heroes, events, and places of Ireland. One famous story involves the origin of the River Boyne, said to be named after the goddess **Boann**, who defied a sacred well's taboo, causing its waters to rise and form the river.

The Dindshenchas is a vital resource for understanding early Irish mythology, geography, and identity, offering a glimpse into how the ancient Irish viewed their world.

Our next stop was the Hill of Tara, and I was truly captivated by this ancient wonder. I had heard so much about its deep historical significance and the ceremonies that once took place there for the High Kings of Ireland. Stepping onto this sacred ground felt like stepping into the heart of Ireland's ancient past, a place where myth and history intertwine.

The Hill of Tara was once the political and spiritual center of ancient Ireland, and it's said that all Irish roads once led here. As we walked up the hill, I couldn't help but think about the countless footsteps that had passed this way over thousands of years—kings, warriors, and perhaps even druids, all gathering for ceremonies that would shape the future of the land.

At the top, we encountered the Lia Fáil, the legendary Stone of Destiny, where Ireland's High Kings were crowned. According to legend, when the rightful king touched the stone, it would cry out in recognition. Standing before this ancient coronation stone, surrounded by the open sky and miles of green countryside, I could almost feel the power and importance this place once held.

The Hill of Tara itself offers a breathtaking panoramic view, stretching out over the lush Irish landscape for miles and miles. From this high vantage point, it's easy to see why this location was chosen for such monumental events. The rolling green fields seemed to go on forever, dotted with farms, small villages, and patches of forest. It was as if the entire history of Ireland could be seen in the landscape below.

The atmosphere on the hill was serene yet filled with a sense of awe, as though the echoes of ancient ceremonies still lingered in the air. It wasn't hard to imagine the High Kings standing here, surveying their lands, surrounded by their people. The Hill of Tara is more than just a historical site—it's a living connection to Ireland's ancient soul, and being there was an experience I won't soon forget. We were allowed to walk across the vast green grass and experience the hill from different angles. It was truly humbling, to say the least.

Next to the Hill of Tara, we discovered a small, charming church and an old cemetery. We were invited to walk along a peaceful path that wound around the cemetery, shaded by towering, ancient trees that seemed to have stood there for centuries, if not thousands of years. The trees, with their thick trunks and sprawling branches, added to the serene, almost mystical atmosphere of the place as if they had witnessed the ebb and flow of Ireland's history alongside the hill itself. Walking beneath them, you couldn't help but feel a deep connection to the past, surrounded by the quiet beauty of both nature and history. I hated to leave and wanted to linger longer, but the tour must continue.

As we boarded the tour bus and made the short journey to Newgrange, there was a sense of quiet anticipation building within me, as though I was about to discover something profound—not just in the landscape, but within myself. We arrived at the visitor center, and before venturing to Newgrange, we spent time exploring the museum. There, we were immersed in the rich history and significance of this ancient site, learning about its creation over 5,000 years ago, its role as a Neolithic passage tomb, and its incredible alignment with the winter solstice. The sense of wonder grew as we absorbed the stories of the people who built it and the mysteries that still surround its purpose.

After walking down a spiraling circular walkway inside the museum, we arrived at a cozy little restaurant on the bottom floor. The menu was simple, offering a small selection of sandwiches and drinks— just enough to recharge before continuing our adventure. We were given about 30 minutes to grab a quick bite, and then we would head out to explore the monument. It was a nice, quiet break before experiencing the awe-inspiring site awaiting us. The restaurant offered a magnificent view of Newgrange, situated just across the river. Sitting there, looking out at the ancient site, the entire experience felt truly humbling—as if we were glimpsing a piece of history that transcended time.

It was a quiet moment of reflection before heading over to experience Newgrange up close.

Our tour guide pointed us toward the bridge leading to Newgrange, where we would board a coach for the short journey to the site. As we made our way through the forest, the air was crisp, and the towering trees provided a natural canopy overhead, adding to the serene atmosphere. Crossing the bridge over the River Boyne was a breathtaking experience. The river, wide and flowing with a powerful yet graceful current, seemed timeless—its waters had likely run this course for thousands of years, just as they had during the ancient days of Newgrange. The sound of the water rushing beneath the bridge added to the sense of connection to the land and history we were about to explore.

We crossed the river and found the coach waiting to take us up to Newgrange. As we drove closer, you could feel the weight of history in the air, like the past was reaching out to meet us. When we disembarked, we walked the short distance up the hill, and there it was—Newgrange, standing before us. The site was massive and awe-inspiring, its ancient presence humbling in a way that made you truly appreciate the thousands of years it has stood there. The excitement of finally being at such a significant place was palpable.

Newgrange is a UNESCO World Heritage Site, and the limited number of visitors allowed inside made the experience feel even more special, as though we were about to be let in on an ancient secret. As we stood before the entrance, gazing at the intricate stone carvings that have survived millennia, I felt a deep connection to something larger than myself. It was as if, at that moment, surrounded by the ancient earth and sky, I had found a piece of my soul—something that had always been there but only now fully realized.

Our tour guide led us into the heart of Newgrange, and as we entered the narrow passage, the ancient stones seemed to close in around us, creating a sense of stepping into another world. When we reached the inner chamber, our guide did something that made the experience even more profound—she turned off all the inside lights, and we were left standing in complete and utter darkness. It was as if time itself stood still. In that stillness, unable to see anything, she explained how, during the winter solstice, a single beam of sunlight enters the tomb, illuminating the inner chamber in a way that must have seemed magical to the ancient people who built it.

Standing in total darkness, our tour guide turned on her flashlight and directed it through where the beam would stream from outside, and it instantly lighted up the entire interior.

For a few moments, we were meant to experience what they had seen—how that single ray of light would pierce the darkness and flood the sacred space with warmth and brightness. It was awe-inspiring to imagine. But then came a little scare—when she turned her flashlight off and went to turn the interior lights back on, there was a brief pause, and we all stood there in the pitch black, wondering if we might be left in that ancient darkness for longer than expected. Finally, the lights flickered back to life, and we laughed with relief as she guided us back out into the daylight.

Once outside, I took my time walking around the massive mound, placing my hand on the smooth, white quartz stones that covered it. I couldn't help but wonder if I might feel something—some connection to the past as if the stones might reveal the stories they had witnessed over millennia. Just like in the movies, I hoped for a spark, some ancient energy to flow through me. But instead, what I felt was even more meaningful—a deep sense of belonging. It was as if, standing there with my hand on those ancient stones, I realized that the connection didn't have to be dramatic or otherworldly. The feeling of being a part of this moment in time, of sharing the same earth as those who built Newgrange, was more than enough. It gave me a sense of peace and contentment that would stay with me, a quiet happiness in knowing that, in some way, we are all connected through time.

Just then, another tour guide shared an astonishing fact: the inside of Newgrange hadn't seen a drop of rain in 5,000 years. It was completely waterproof, just as it had been since the day it was built. He also mentioned that soon, the site would no longer be called Newgrange, as it was returning to its original name, *Brú na Bóinne.*

With that, he led us back to the coach that would take us to the museum, where we reboarded the tour bus to head back to Dublin.

This had to be one of the most fulfilling days of my life. The entire experience was deeply moving, and I could feel the weight of history in my bones. Despite my legs aching from all the walking and climbing, I felt nothing but a calm sense of peace, like I had touched something timeless and profound.

The ride back to Dublin began with light chatter but soon gave way to a peaceful silence as everyone settled into their own thoughts. I pulled out my notebook, eager to capture every detail of the experience while it was still fresh in my mind. The quiet on the bus felt reflective, almost as if each person was processing the same profound emotions I was. Whether they were tired or simply absorbed in the gravity of the day, the mood was serene.

We had just visited, learned about, and explored a site built thousands of years ago by ancient hands, and the weight of that history felt humbling. There was a deep connection to the past, a sense of standing in the footsteps of our ancestors, and it left a mark on me that I knew would last a lifetime. As we made our way back to the modern city of Dublin, I couldn't help but reflect on how incredible it was to witness something so timeless, something that spoke of humanity's enduring spirit.

It wasn't long before the bus pulled back up to Ned Kelly's, and we grabbed our backpacks and disembarked. The contrast between the gentle and quiet rolling hills and the huge megalithic sites to the bustling streets of Dublin was surreal. I knew then that I would return to Newgrange one day. I will tell everyone I know about the profound experience I had that day and how it changed my point of view of the past and its people. The history of Ireland is so extensive and incredible, and I know there are many people who do not know this history, and that saddens me.

After calling a cab, we headed off to what promised to be another incredible adventure. I had booked two nights at a real castle—Clontarf Castle. I had seen a photo of a stunning mural located in one of the castle's bars, and from that moment, I knew it was the place I wanted to stay. The castle was a surprise gift for Christina, and I was certain she would love it. This was going to be a magical experience!

The mural in Clontarf Castle Hotel in Dublin, Ireland, is in the Great Hall and Knight's Bar. It vividly depicts the famous Battle of Clontarf. This historic battle fought in 1014, saw the Irish High King Brian Boru defeat the Viking invaders. Clontarf Castle was built in 1172 and is steeped in history, with centuries of stories unfolding within its walls. The castle's name, "Clontarf," originates from the sound of the sea rolling over the sandbanks in Dublin Bay, a reminder of its deep connection to both the land and its legendary past.

We arrived at Clontarf Castle and were instantly in awe of its towering, majestic structure, surrounded by perfectly manicured gardens. The castle, often used for weddings, also attracts guests from all over the world who come to marvel at the incredible artifacts on display throughout. From high-backed king's chairs to grand chandeliers and portraits of former lords, every corner was a spectacle of history and elegance.

Our room was on the third floor, beautifully updated with modern amenities but still retaining the ambiance of a castle room. It was a hotel, yet it carried that regal charm you'd expect from such a historic place. After quickly freshening up, Christina, Angela, and I headed down to the Knight's Bar to see the famous mural and grab a pint. By now, we had fully embraced the Irish way—no longer just having a drink but "grabbing a pint." Ireland was rubbing off on us.

When we finally found the bar and laid eyes on the mural, it took our breath away. Carved directly into the granite wall, it vividly depicted the Battle of Clontarf, the momentous victory where King Brian Boru defeated the Vikings. The detail and artistry of the mural, combined with the history it represented, were truly awe-inspiring. It was a sight that felt both timeless and unforgettable.

It had been a long day full of emotion and wonder, so we decided to eat at the bar and then call it a night. The Knights Bar at Clontarf Castle was nothing short of enchanting—a space that feels like stepping into a storybook steeped in history and grandeur. The room is a masterpiece of Gothic elegance, with its high vaulted ceilings, intricately carved woodwork, and stately chandeliers casting a warm, golden glow. The walls are adorned with rich tapestries and coats of arms, whispering tales of knights and nobility from a bygone era.

Every detail feels regal yet inviting, from the plush seating to the polished oak bar, where skilled bartenders craft drinks with effortless charm. The atmosphere hums with a sense of timelessness, where echoes of medieval feasts seem to blend seamlessly with the murmur of modern conversations. Sipping a drink here, surrounded by the castle's mystique, feels like being part of something magical, a moment suspended between past and present.

While we were waiting on our food, we saw something that made us smile—a true Texan walked in, sporting a 10-gallon hat and cowboy boots. We struck up a conversation with him, exchanging pleasantries and learning he was from Fort Worth, traveling with his wife. Both of them, elderly and full of life, seemed to be thoroughly enjoying their time in Ireland.

Angela, Christina, and I placed our dinner orders at the Knights Bar—Angela and I chose the steak, while Christina went for the Irish stew. When the food arrived, it looked incredible, but I found my appetite had faded. The exhaustion of the day caught up with me, leaving me too tired and introspective to enjoy the meal fully. Our cucumber Chilton, however, was refreshing, and I managed to finish mine and ordered another. As Angela and Christina chatted about the day's adventures, their voices became a soft background to my thoughts. I found myself lost in quiet reflection, processing all we had seen and experienced, barely tuned into the lively conversation at the bar.

It had been a long day, but in the best way possible—fulfilling and deeply meaningful. Eventually, I excused myself and headed upstairs to the room, feeling the need to put pen to paper and capture the emotions and thoughts swirling in my head. It truly had been an amazing day, and the journey wasn't over yet. I felt an overwhelming sense of gratitude for this trip and for all the incredible experiences it had brought.

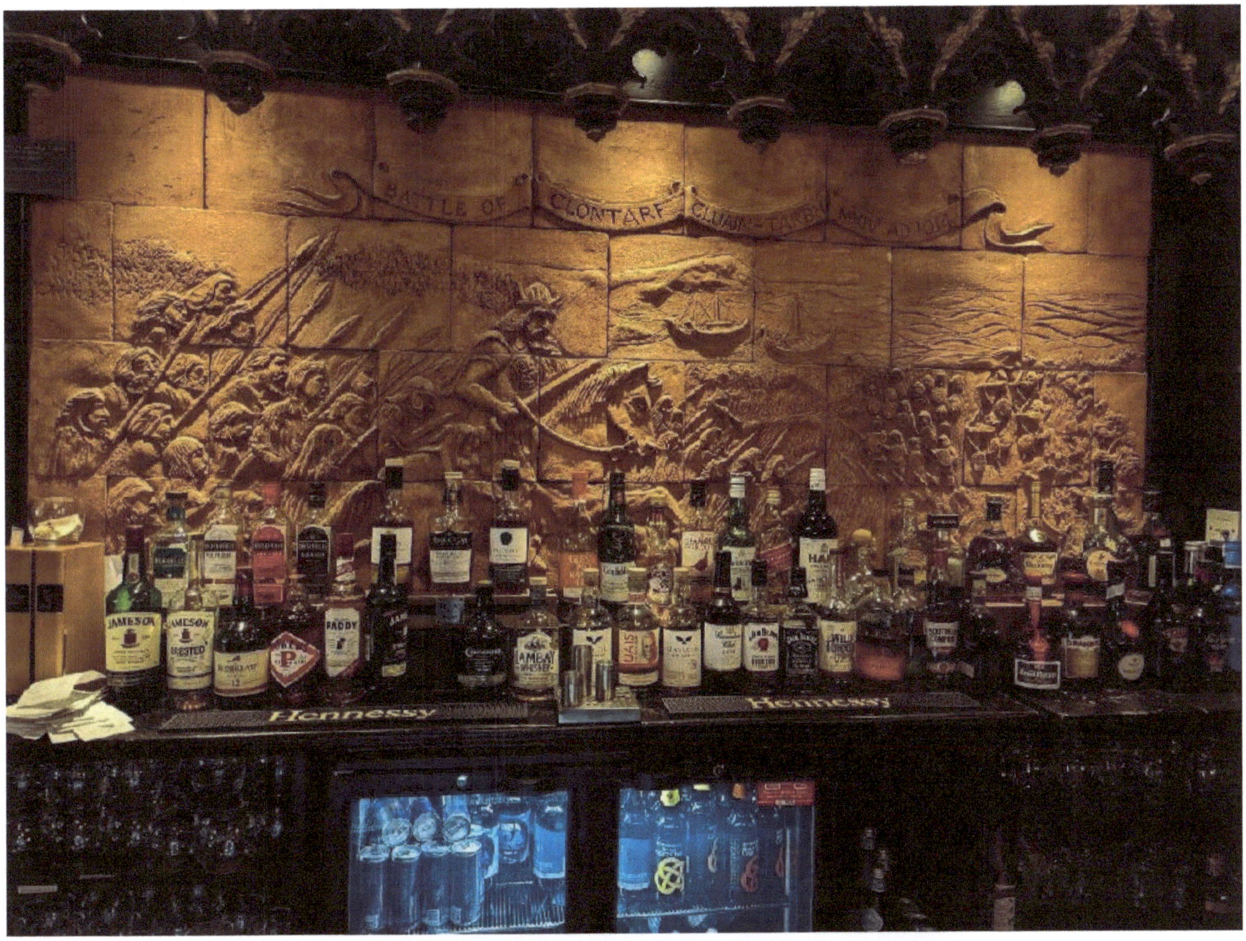
BATTLE OF CLONTARF
JAMESON
Hennessy
Hennessy

PUSH

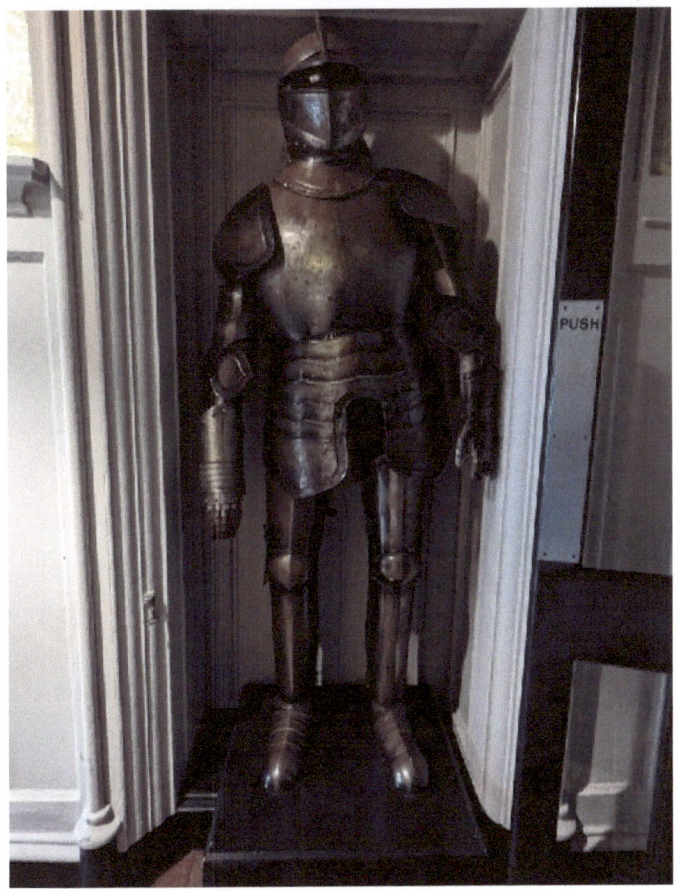

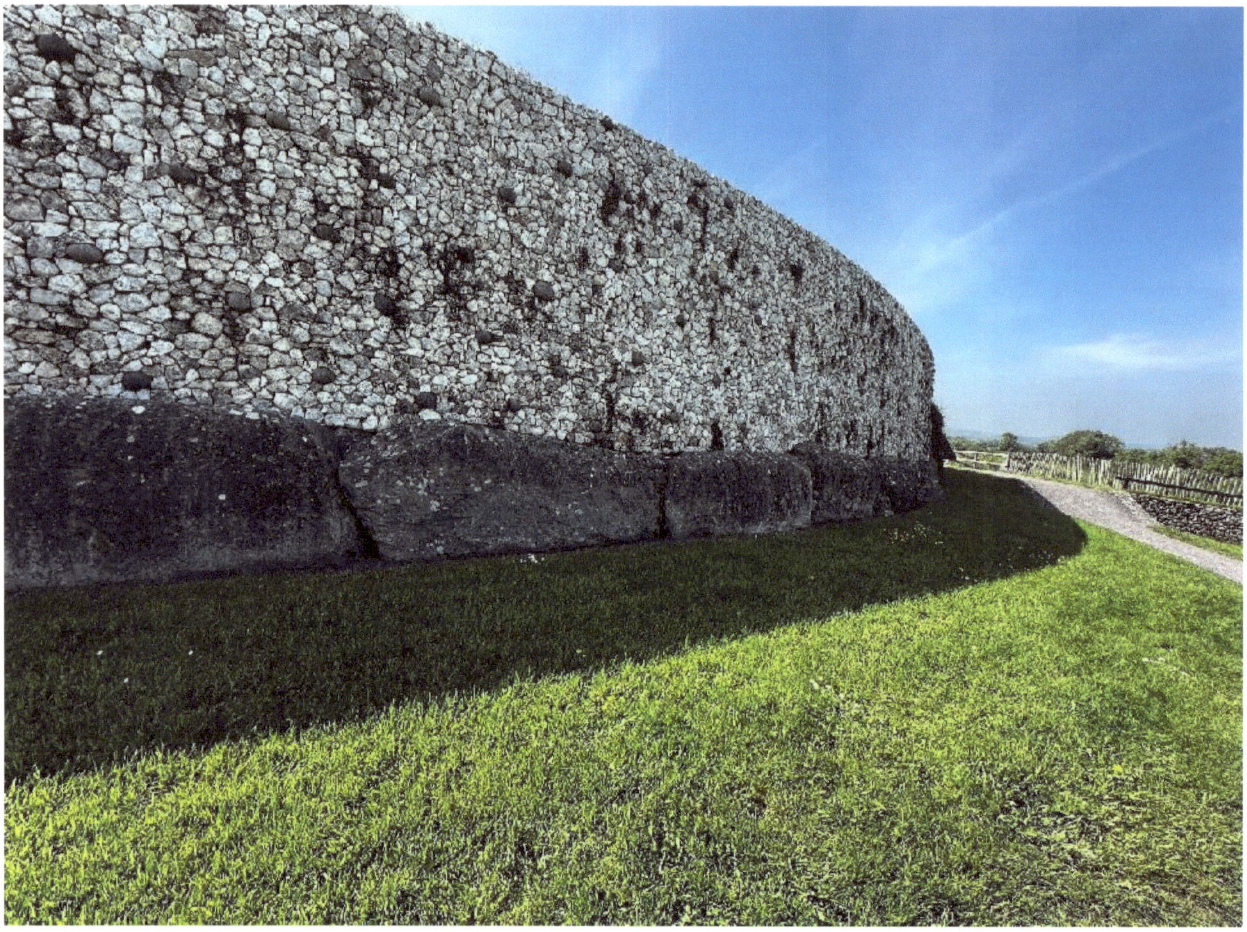

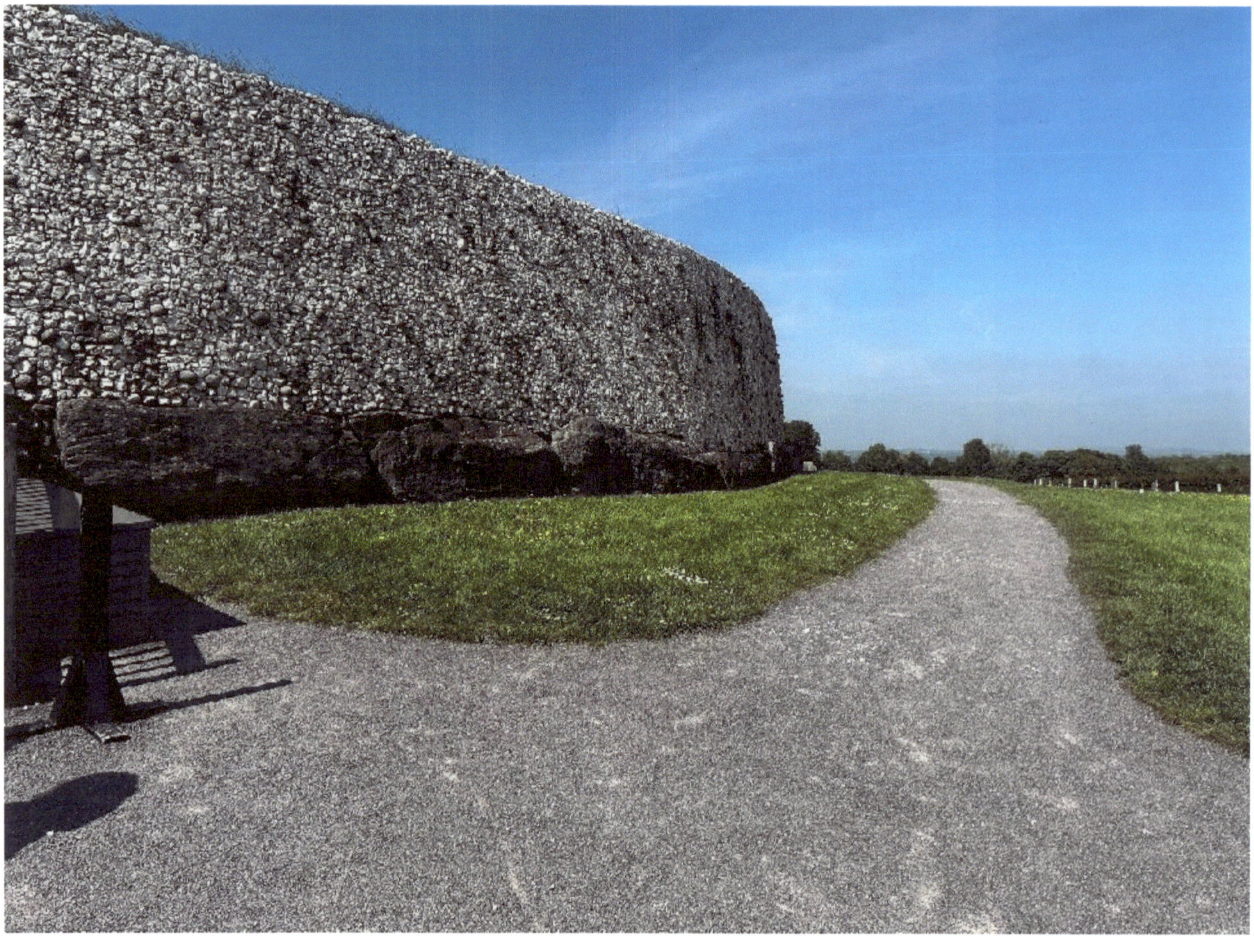

CHAPTER SIX: SEANS BAR & TRAINS

Day 4:

We woke up to another beautiful sunny day in Ireland, something the locals assured us was a rare treat. Today was the day we'd be taking the train to Athlone to visit Sean's Bar, the oldest bar in Ireland, as confirmed by the Guinness Book of World Records. The excitement was building for the 1 ½ hour train ride there and back—I couldn't wait to finally see Sean's Bar in person. It had come up time and time again in my research, popping up on several media sites. I wasn't sure what it said about us that we were so eager to visit the oldest bar in Ireland (and possibly the world!), but I didn't care. It was going to be amazing to travel by train for the first time and visit a bar that had been standing since the year 900, during the Viking Age.

Before setting off, we took some time to explore the remarkable Clontarf Castle. The castle's rich history was evident in every detail, from the intricate stonework to the grand hallways adorned with artifacts and large, imposing portraits of past occupants. These paintings seemed to watch over the castle, a reminder of the centuries of stories contained within its walls. The atmosphere was steeped in history, with every room offering a glimpse into the lives of those who had called the castle home.

Eventually, our wanderings brought us back to the present, and we made our way down to the elegant restaurant for breakfast. The dining room maintained the castle's timeless charm while offering modern comforts, with its cozy ambiance and attentive staff setting the perfect tone for the morning.

Breakfast was nothing short of astonishing. It was a massive spread, featuring everything from freshly baked scones to the traditional black pudding. I had never seen so much food in one place! The Irish really know how to do breakfast, and every meal so far had been an adventure in itself. The impressive layout made it easy to try a little bit of everything, and I happily indulged, fueling up for what I knew was going to be an unforgettable day.

After finishing our incredible breakfast, we asked the front desk staff how to get to the train station. They explained that first, we'd walk to the corner, catch a bus, then hop on a tram, and finally, we'd arrive at Heuston Station (yes, it's pronounced "Houston"). The process sounded like quite an adventure, and my excitement was building. We could have called for a cab, but we wanted to experience the people. What better way than through transportation?

It didn't take us long to walk to the bus stop, where we boarded a packed bus full of charming folks making their way to work or wherever. We rode the bus for a few minutes until we departed and got on a tram, which was quite an adventure. The tram ride in Dublin was a perfect blend of modern convenience and urban charm. Sleek and efficient, the tram glided smoothly along its tracks, weaving through the bustling streets of the city. The large windows offered panoramic views of Dublin's vibrant life—historic buildings standing proudly alongside contemporary architecture, busy sidewalks filled with locals and tourists, and flashes of greenery in parks and gardens.

Inside, the atmosphere was lively yet orderly, with a mix of commuters heading to work or school, groups of friends chatting, and visitors like us studying the route map with curiosity. The rhythmic hum of the tram and the occasional automated announcements added to the experience, creating a sense of both movement and connection to the city. It was more than just transportation—it was a window into the daily pulse of Dublin, a moment to observe and feel part of its dynamic energy.

We reached the train station in about 30 minutes, but those 30 minutes felt as if I'd lived in Dublin my entire life. If you ever have the chance to ride a bus or tram in Dublin, take it. It's more than just a way to get around—it's an enjoyable experience that lets you connect with the city's rhythm and the energy of its people.

I have always loved to people-watch, and using a city's transportation system lets you see the people up close and personal. The elderly Irish seemed to have a thick melodic accent with phrases like "Ah sure, isn't it grand?" Older men wear a neatly pressed flat cap and tweed jacket, while elderly women always wear a scarf and have a purse in their lap. The younger crowd is a bit easier to understand with their polished and crisp accents. Many of the younger people have only a slight hint of an accent, which would make me believe that their brogue was softened by education. Many of the younger people dress exactly like the younger people in America. They wear smartwatches and blue jeans and carry backpacks everywhere they go.

You can always tell who the tourists are. Those are the people who are wearing t-shirts emblazoned with "Ireland" in bold green letters, carrying maps and guidebooks.

The elderly and their thick accent are the first to exchange pleasantries with Americans. Their words tumble out with warmth and humor, and they are often the first to engage, whereas the younger Irish seem to be caught up in their own little worlds.

There were a couple of people that were most interesting to me. Two nuns riding the tram to the train station. Both sounded Irish but were very soft-spoken, making it hard to hear. Where I live in the desert southwest of the States, I don't see many nuns, so seeing and hearing them on the tram was most exciting to me.

I had never been to a train station before, and as we approached Heuston Station, a mix of nerves and anticipation hit me. The station was buzzing with activity—people coming and going in every direction. My anxiety was increasing rapidly from all the excitement. The noise level was high, with the hum of conversations, the announcements over the speakers, and the sounds of trains pulling in and out. It felt like I had stepped into the Edgar Allan Poe story "The Man of the Crowd," where the energy of the people around me brought the station to life. It was thrilling to be part of the movement, but it was also a little nerve-racking for someone unfamiliar with train stations. The environment was thrilling and scary at the same time.

We found the train that would take us to Athlone and realized we had a short wait. Naturally, we decided to check out the local pub conveniently located right inside the train station. Can you believe they had a pub right inside the train station? Have I mentioned how much I love Ireland? Haha. After a couple of drinks and some lively conversation with the locals, it was time to board.

Excitement bubbled up as we walked down the platform, passing several open doors before reaching our assigned one. For some reason, I had assumed we would board through the first open door and walk through the entire train to find our seats, even if it meant passing through multiple cars. I guess my idea came from movies, where that always seems to be how train stations work!

As we boarded, I quickly realized my seat wasn't in the same section as Christina and Angela. No worries, though—I had writing to do! I settled into my seat, pulled out my notebook, and started recording the day's adventures. Soon enough, the train began to pull out of the station, and the rhythmic clackity-clack of the rails brought me out of my thoughts. I glanced out the window, curious to take in the view. Sitting in a four-seat booth with no one else around, I had no distractions.

As we left downtown Dublin and headed west toward Athlone, the cityscape gave way to miles of lush green countryside. Everywhere I looked, vibrant shades of green stretched as far as the eye could see. This truly is the Emerald Isle, and the beauty of the landscape was captivating. The train made several stops along the way, with passengers getting on and off at each one, and the conversations around me were lively and cheerful.

I had planned to do more writing, but I couldn't tear myself away from the window. Watching the rolling hills and fields pass by was too much fun. Riding the train was an adventure in itself, and I found myself completely absorbed in the journey, soaking in the beauty of Ireland.

The closer we got to Athlone, the more I noticed tiny raindrops splattering against the window. By the time we arrived, a gentle rain was falling steadily, creating that classic Irish atmosphere. We hadn't thought to bring umbrellas, but we didn't care—we were too excited! When we arrived in Athlone, the rain was coming down harder. But we toughed it out, laughing as we walked the few blocks to Sean's Bar, rain soaking us through. Our hair was plastered on our heads, and any attempt at looking put together had been washed away by the raindrops, but we were in good spirits, enjoying the adventure.

As we strolled through the rainy streets, we passed a large, round castle right in the middle of town. It was Athlone Castle. Athlone Castle is a striking historical landmark situated on the banks of the River Shannon in the heart of Athlone. Its massive stone walls and round towers immediately transport you back in time. The castle was originally built as a strategic fortress in the 12th century. The castle's imposing presence dominates the town, serving as both a defensive stronghold and a symbol of power through the ages. At that time, the castle was closed, but we could walk around the outside and marvel at its size and read the placards strategically placed. As we walked around the massive castle, we realized something amazing—we were standing right outside of Sean's Bar! It looked just like the photos I had seen online, a charming and welcoming sight despite the weather. We exchanged huge smiles, excitement bubbling up as we headed toward the entrance. Wet and happy, we were ready to step inside and experience the oldest bar in Ireland!

The old wooden door with the stained-glass window reading Sean's Bar in bold multicolored letters creaked as we opened it. We were immediately greeted by the warm, cozy atmosphere of a truly Irish pub. On our right, a fireplace crackled with a comforting fire, its stone hearth looking like it had been burning for centuries. The entryway was simple, with a scattering of small tables and chairs and booths lining the wall. To the left, toward the middle of the room, was the main bar, its shelves lined with Irish whiskey bottles and taps serving draft beer.

Along the right-hand wall, prominently displayed, was the Guinness World Records certificate, officially recognizing Sean's Bar as the oldest bar in Ireland—and quite possibly the oldest bar still standing in the world. The certificate was mounted in front of a section of the wall that had been standing since 900 A.D. It was surreal to be in a place with such history. We admired the old photos that adorned both walls, capturing moments of the bar's long and storied past.

At the end of the room, another door opened into a second entryway with restrooms. Beyond that, another door led to a large, covered area filled with more tables and bars. Though it was enclosed, we could hear the soft patter of rain on the covering and see the raindrops dance as they hit the roof. It was the perfect spot to enjoy a pint while soaking in the sounds of the Irish rain.

After wandering for a bit and admiring our surroundings, we returned to the main bar and ordered a couple of pints, then made our way to the rear bar to enjoy the ambiance and the gentle sound of the rain. To our surprise, Timmy, the owner of the bar, walked in to greet us. I had seen him in interviews all over the internet, chatting with people from Canada, America, France, China, and even Russia and anyone else who would listen about the history of Sean's Bar. He was incredibly friendly and charming, making us feel instantly welcomed as his customers.

I asked if we could take a picture with him, and he happily agreed. Angela took the photo with Christina and me on either side of Timmy, grinning despite being soaked to the bone. It was a fantastic picture, capturing the moment perfectly—us looking like drowned rats but thrilled, nonetheless. We chatted with Timmy for another 30 minutes or so before another customer caught his attention. What a genuinely lovely guy!

We finished a couple more pints and, still buzzing with happiness, made our way back to the train station. The rain had let up slightly, but it was still drizzling as we arrived at the small station and boarded the train back to Dublin. Once again, my seat was separated from Christina's and Angela's. But there were open seats next to them that hadn't been taken, so we all sat together anyway. I sat with them until someone came to claim their seat, at which point I'd have to move—always good for a laugh!

Eventually, someone did come to claim their seat—a cute young blonde Irish girl. I scooted over across the aisle to let her in, and she quickly pulled out her laptop, engrossed in her work. But something soon caught her attention—Christina was trying to start a conversation with her. At first, the girl seemed oblivious to her surroundings, but then she tuned in to Christina's words. Her first response was, "Are you American?" Christina enthusiastically replied, "Yes!"

The girl's name was Elmear, though it took us a moment to figure out how to pronounce it. Once the introductions were made, she happily chatted with us for the rest of the ride back to Dublin. Elmear told us she was born and raised in the area and that her parents owned a farm in central Ireland. She was attending school in Dublin and would be graduating soon. Recently, she took a trip to New York, and she couldn't get over the accents there, but she found them fascinating.

When she asked Angela about her accent, Elmear was surprised to learn that we were from Texas. Her eyes lit up, and she and Angela dove into conversation, chatting away about all the things young women love to talk about—school, travel, and life in general. It was amazing to watch two young women from completely different worlds, yet so similar in many ways, carry on such a lively conversation. Despite living miles apart, they shared so much in common, and their connection was a lovely reminder of how small the world can be.

As Angela and Eimear continued their cheerful conversation, I returned to people-watching and jotting down notes about the surroundings. At each train stop on our way back to Dublin, passengers came and went—people from all walks of life. I couldn't help but wonder what some of them did for a living, especially as we passed through small towns that seemed so quiet and modest. It would have been fascinating to step off the train and explore one of those little villages, if only for a while.

Next time I visit Ireland, I think I'll take a different approach. Instead of relying solely on trains, I'll rent a car and explore some of these small towns, stopping to chat with the locals and soak in their stories. There's something deeply captivating about a place so steeped in history and enchantment—it's the kind of life I'd love to experience, even if just for a little while.

We arrived back in Dublin and started wandering through the streets on our way back to Clontarf Castle. Just walking through the streets of Dublin was a humbling experience, with the combination of old buildings set against the buzz of new technology.

Along the way, Christina spotted another wonderful place to eat—The Yacht Bar and Restaurant. The bar was absolutely charming, with its nautical theme inspired by Dublin Bay, which lay just outside, offering beautiful views of the water. The atmosphere felt cozy yet vibrant, the perfect spot to unwind after our busy day.

We all ordered the steak with chips (which are just French fries) and onion rings. Christina and I ordered a tall cranberry and vodka. All was delicious. Angela, on the other hand, opted for a playful drink that was quite the showstopper. It came with a long straw, star-shaped pineapple slices, and a tall, full-bodied glass topped with what looked like fluffy orange foam. To top it all off, there was an adorable little pear bear perched on the rim. It was fun and whimsical, adding to the joy of the evening.

For dessert, we decided to indulge and share a selection of treats. Apple pie, ice cream, a warm brownie, more scoops of ice cream, and delicate wafers. Each bite was better than the last, and we couldn't stop smiling and laughing as we dug in. It was the perfect ending to an already wonderful day, and we left feeling both full and incredibly happy.

If you're looking for great restaurant recommendations in Dublin, the Yacht Bar & Restaurant should be at the top of your list. The staff are incredibly helpful and friendly, the food is locally sourced and absolutely delicious, and the prices are surprisingly affordable. And don't forget about the stunning picturesque views of Dublin Bay.

After dinner, we took a leisurely stroll down the promenade along Dublin Bay. It was peaceful and charming, the perfect way to unwind after a big meal and a long, exciting day. The soft sound of the water and the cool evening breeze made the walk feel serene, allowing us to fully appreciate the moment. Once we had soaked in the beauty of the bay, we headed back to Clontarf Castle, content and happy.

Reflecting on the day, it felt like one of those rare, perfect days that would forever hold a special place in my memory. We took a train ride through lush green landscapes and shimmering raindrops as we explored Athlone Castle, the unforgettable stop at Sean's Bar, where we met the wonderful Timmy and the lively conversation with Elmear on the train ride back. Then, there was the delicious food and playful drinks at The Yacht Bar, followed by the calming walk along the bay.

As we approached the castle, I was filled with gratitude for such an incredible day. Christina and I decided to stop in the hotel bar for a nightcap while Angela headed up to the room. After our lovely nightcap, we made our way to the room to bring an end to what had truly been a magical day in Dublin, Ireland. Everything about it—the experiences, the views, the food, and the company—had left me feeling completely fulfilled.

The past four days in Dublin had flown by, and the thought of leaving tomorrow filled me with sadness. This city truly captured my heart, and one thing I know for certain is that I will return. If you ever get the chance to visit Ireland, make sure Dublin is on your list. The city is filled with wonderful people and countless amazing sights to explore. Every cab ride, train journey, and bus trip revealed the warmth, kindness, and generosity of the locals. Dublin's charm is unmatched, and one day, I'll come back to experience it all over again—of that, you can be sure.

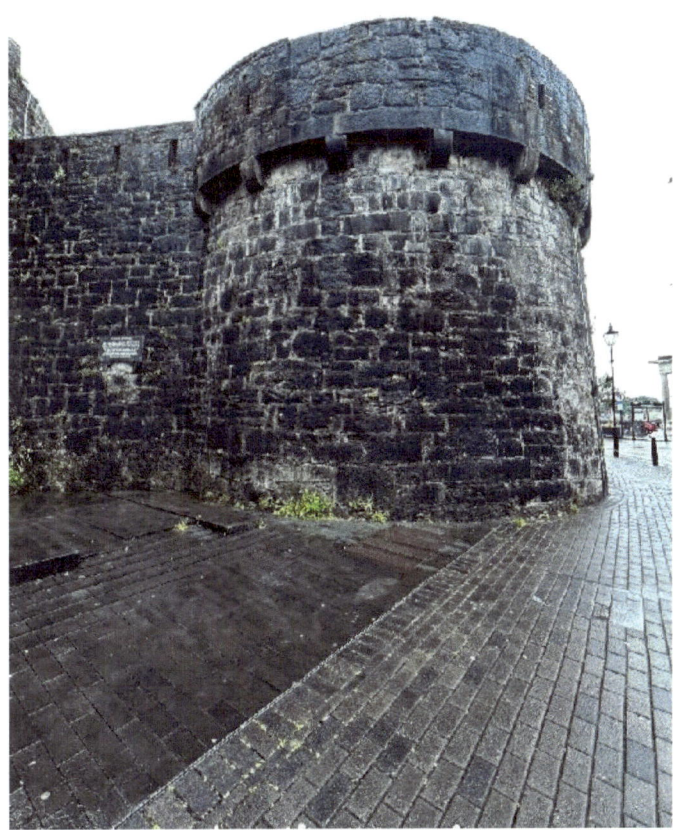

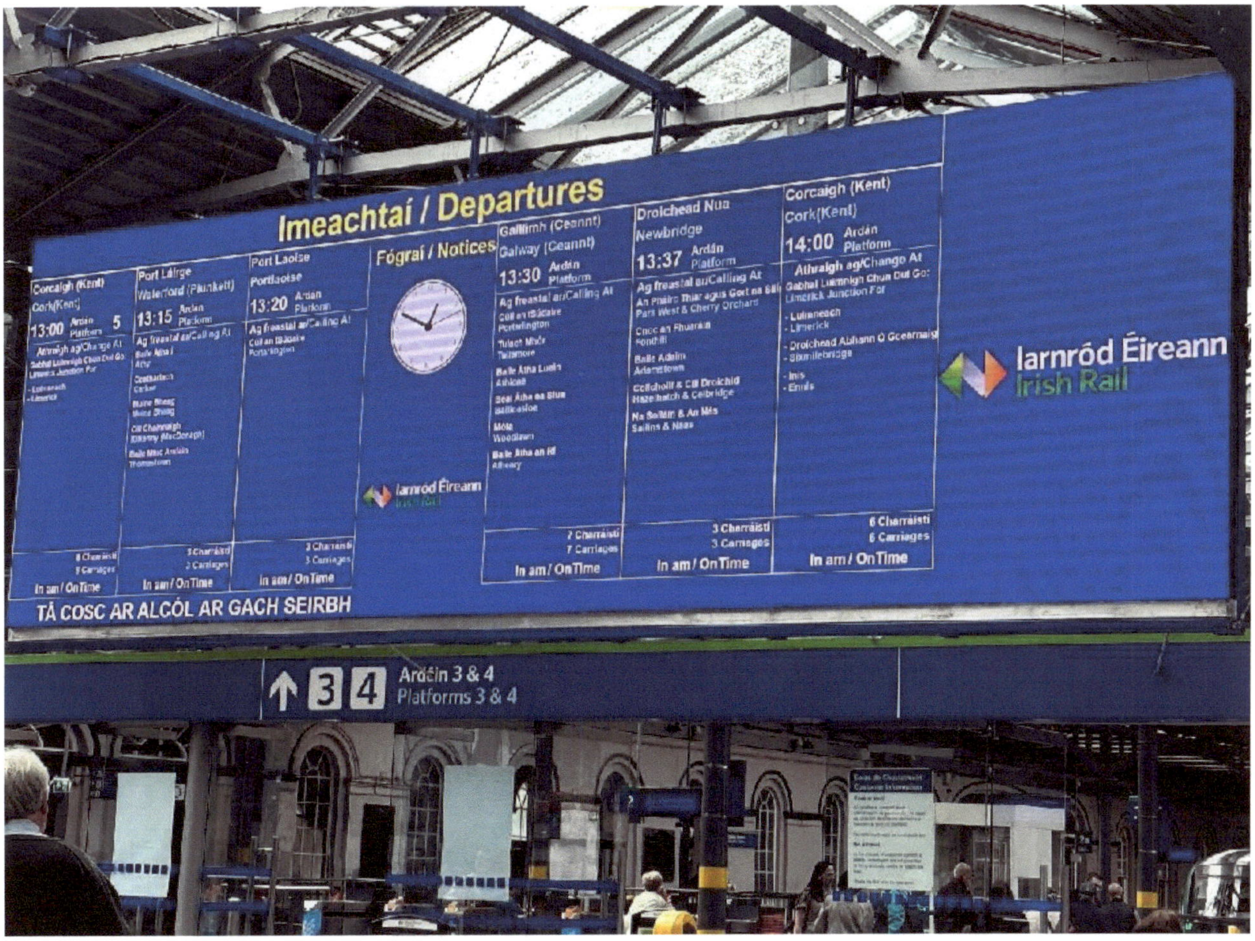
Imeachtaí / Departures
Fógraí / Notices
Gaillimh (Ceannt)
Galway (Ceannt)
13:30
Droichead Nua
Newbridge
13:37
Corcaigh (Kent)
Cork(Kent)
14:00
In am / OnTime
Iarnród Éireann
Irish Rail
TÁ COSC AR ALCÓL AR GACH SEIRBH
3 4
Ardáin 3 & 4
Platforms 3 & 4

CHAPTER SEVEN: GALWAY & SPAIN

Day 5:

I must mention the two housekeepers at Clontarf Castle Hotel and how utterly charming they were. Day 5 marked our final moments in Dublin, and saying goodbye was bittersweet, especially as we parted ways with the hotel staff. The two elderly housekeepers, embodying quintessential Irish warmth and old-world charm, left a lasting impression on me. They were brimming with curiosity about America, asking us thoughtful questions, and in return, they shared an abundance of stories about Ireland. Their voices carried a deep sense of pride and nostalgia, making our farewell all the more memorable. I cannot for the life of me remember their names. I wish I had jotted their names down, but they were the most gracious people I have ever met in my life. Dublin and all of Ireland should be very proud of these two women and the pride they have for their country. I did write a short note and handed it to the hotel receptionist, giving them praise for such great work. I hope that they were able to see the kind words and to know how much they touched us during our stay.

Interacting with those in the service industry often leaves me reflecting deeply on their essential role in shaping a travel experience. Tourists are profoundly impacted by the dedication and kindness of these hardworking individuals, many of whom are hourly employees. It's important to approach every interaction with respect and gratitude, whether in America, Ireland, or anywhere else in the world.

Hotel staff, restaurant servers, bus and cab drivers, guides at national monuments—anyone connected to the tourism industry—holds the power to enhance or diminish a visitor's impression of a country. During my stay in Ireland, the staff at Clontarf Castle stood out for their exceptional warmth and helpfulness. I can only hope the people of Ireland recognize what a gift these individuals are to visitors like me.

As we made our way back to Heuston Station, the weight of leaving Dublin settled in, but there was excitement, too, for what lay ahead. Our next destination was Galway, a two-and-a-half-hour train ride away—just enough time to sit quietly, write, and reflect. I opened my journal, eager to capture every detail, every emotion. I knew these memories would be treasures to return to long after the journey was over. The city was behind us now, but its stories and the people we met would stay with me forever.

We made it to the train station just in time to catch our train to Galway. As we settled in, something caught my attention that I hadn't noticed on our previous journey—a language over the intercom that I'd never heard before. I was intrigued, and a lovely lady nearby explained it was Gaelic. The conductor would announce everything in Gaelic first, followed by English. There was even a running display onboard, printing out the announcements in both languages. How cool was that! I found myself captivated, watching the words on the sign, listening for the differences and similarities between Gaelic and English. Some words seemed so different, yet others had a familiar rhythm. Curious.

Once we found our seats, I realized the train was completely full. This time, we were lucky—all of our seats were together, and I was impressed to see our names displayed above our section. Such a thoughtful organization! We talked excitedly amongst ourselves, planning out our time in Galway getting everything in order. But soon, the beautiful scenery outside the window stole our attention. Every station we passed had signs in both Gaelic and English, which I thought was amazing—a reminder of the blend of old and new in this place.

I couldn't believe how very fast time went by, and it wasn't long before we arrived in Galway, ready to begin another adventure, our curiosity and excitement carrying us forward.

During my research on Galway, I discovered fascinating details about its rich history. Once a bustling Spanish port, Galway has long been a gateway to the world. Its maritime heritage is deeply intertwined with its identity, and its connection to Spain is still felt in the city today. The heart of Galway is Eyre Square, a lively and historic space that has seen centuries of change. It's hard to imagine that Christopher Columbus himself once walked through this very square, a testament to the city's enduring role in global exploration.

Eyre Square sits at the center of Galway's vibrant culture, alive with buskers, markets, and the energy of locals and visitors alike. It's also a key point along the famous Wild Atlantic Way, a stunning coastal route that displays the rugged beauty of Ireland's western shores. The more I learned about Galway, the more I understood its importance—not just as a city but as a place where history, culture, and nature converge. I couldn't wait to see it all for myself.

We arrived in Galway around 1 pm and made our way to the Eyre Square Hotel, which Christina had found during her part of the research project. Situated directly across from the bustling Eyre Square, the main hub of the town, the hotel had a charming atmosphere. Its restaurant had an elegant, antique feel, and the staff greeted us with warmth and friendliness. Though we couldn't check in until 3 pm, they kindly offered to watch our backpacks while we explored the square and its many attractions.

Feeling a bit hungry, we decided to trust Christina's restaurant expertise once again. She picked a delightful little Italian spot called Gatto Rosso, right in Eyre Square. The cozy restaurant was filled with Italian charm, its theme centering around red cats, which added a quirky and inviting touch. We all tried different Italian dishes, which were delightful and tasty. I sampled the Bolognese while Christina opted for a Margherita pizza. Angela decided on the carbonara Spaghetti. We also tried different delightful drinks and different glasses of wine. A perfect start to our afternoon.

After our delicious meal, we set off to explore the city, weaving through the many shops and stores that lined the streets. As the rain began to fall intermittently, we made a quick stop to buy umbrellas, embracing the Irish weather as we continued our wandering.

One of our first stops, in Eyre Square, was the bust of John F. Kennedy—a symbol of the lasting connection between Ireland and the U.S. Sometimes Eyre Square is mentioned as John F Kennedy Park or Kennedy Memorial Park, the formal name given to Eyre Square in his honor. The bust and accompanying plaque commemorate Kennedy's visit to Ireland and his speech in Galway, where he expressed admiration for the Irish people and their contribution to the world.

In Eyre Square, there was also the Browne Doorway. The Browne House doorway is a striking and historic architectural feature that captures the essence of the city's medieval charm. This ornately carved doorway once belonged to the Browne family, one of Galway's influential "Tribes"—the 14 merchant families who dominated the city's trade and politics during the medieval period. The doorway is framed with intricate stone carvings, showcasing late Gothic and Renaissance influences. Floral motifs, heraldic symbols, and decorative patterns highlight the craftsmanship of the era.

We then headed over to the Galway Museum, where we learned so much about the city's fascinating history. The Galway City Museum is a treasure trove of history, culture, and storytelling, nestled in the heart of Galway, just steps away from the Spanish Arch. From the moment you step inside, you're greeted by an inviting blend of modern design and historic charm, with bright, open spaces that guide you through Ireland's rich past and vibrant present.

The museum's exhibits span centuries, from ancient archaeological finds to tales of medieval Galway, the maritime heritage of the region, and its role in Ireland's fight for independence. Each display is thoughtfully curated, blending artifacts, multimedia installations, and personal stories that bring history to life.

One highlight is the stunning views from the upper floors, where large windows frame the River Corrib and Galway Bay, a reminder of the city's enduring connection to the sea. The museum feels intimate yet expansive, offering visitors a chance to immerse themselves in Galway's spirit, culture, and resilience. It's more than just a museum—it's a gateway to understanding the heart of this remarkable city.

While at the museum, we learned something very exciting. Galway was once home to survivors of the sunken Spanish Armada, though tragically, many of them met a grim fate as they were reportedly killed upon reaching the Irish shores due to strained relations between the Irish and Spanish at the time. There was also an intriguing legend tied to the fate of some of the Spanish Armada's crewmen. After the ships wrecked off the Irish coast, it's said that not all of the survivors faced the grim end that history records.

Some of the Spanish sailors, rather than risk capture or execution by the Spanish government for abandoning their posts, quietly disappeared into the vast Irish population. They mingled with the local people, blending into the rural communities and starting new lives far from the reach of Spanish authorities. Over time, these men are believed to have married into Irish families, their Spanish bloodline weaving itself into the fabric of Irish society.

The idea that their descendants still walk the streets of Galway adds a sense of mystery and romance to the city, with whispers of a hidden connection between Ireland and Spain that runs deeper than the historical records suggest. You can almost feel it in the vibrant mix of cultures, from the architecture to the food and music, as if a part of that Spanish influence still lingers in the air. The legend gave the city a sense of intrigue that added to its already captivating charm.

We also learned about the Spanish Arch, a significant landmark that holds a deep connection between Ireland and Spain. This lone arch is one of the few remnants of Galway's medieval past and stands as a symbol of the city's maritime history. Built-in 1584, it was originally part of the city's defensive walls, designed to protect the bustling port from invaders and safeguard the trade routes that linked Galway to the rest of the world, especially Spain.

During the height of Galway's prominence as a Spanish port, ships from Spain would dock nearby, unloading goods and supplies and contributing to the rich cultural exchange between the two nations. The Spanish Arch, overlooking the River Corrib, was once a gateway for these vessels, a critical point of commerce and trade. Its name reflects the deep bond Galway shared with Spain, a connection not only through trade but also in culture and people.

Standing before it, you can feel the weight of history, imagining the Spanish galleons arriving, the sailors disembarking, and the goods being traded on the bustling waterfront. Though time has eroded much of the old walls, the Spanish Arch endures, a silent witness to centuries of history, from its early days guarding the port to its current role as a reminder of Galway's ties to Spain. It's a symbol of the city's enduring relationship with the sea and the cultural bridges it has built over time.

Just a short walk from the Spanish Arch is Galway's vibrant Latin Quarter, an area steeped in history and buzzing with energy. The Latin Quarter is filled with narrow, cobblestone streets, colorful storefronts, and an abundance of lively pubs, cafes, and shops. It's a place where Galway's past and present collide, and the Spanish influence lingers. The area is known for its street performers, traditional Irish music, and a festival-like atmosphere, offering a sensory experience with the aroma of freshly brewed coffee, hearty Irish stews, and, of course, pints of Guinness.

As we wandered through the Latin Quarter, we felt the echoes of Galway's maritime past in the architecture and cultural touches throughout. From the Spanish Arch to the bustling streets of the Latin Quarter, the Spanish influence is woven into the very fabric of this lively city, a reminder of Galway's unique place in the history of Ireland and its connections to the wider world.

As Christina and I wandered through the lively streets of the Latin Quarter, Angela, who had been off exploring on a rent-a-bike, found us, and we decided it was time for a warm break. The west coast of Ireland, with its bracing Atlantic winds, was noticeably cooler than the east, and we could feel the chill settling into our bones. Christina, with her knack for finding the perfect spots to eat or drink, led us to a charming little shop where we ordered hot chocolate and a scone.

We found a seat outside, bundled up against the cool air, and settled in to watch the world go by. The warmth of the hot chocolate in our hands felt like pure comfort, and the scones were just the right mix of sweet and hearty. As we sat, the Latin Quarter buzzed with life around us—locals and tourists mingling, street performers playing traditional Irish tunes, and the rhythm of Galway pulsing through the narrow, cobblestone streets. It was one of those perfect moments where everything felt just right, the simple joy of good company and a warm drink making us feel fulfilled and connected to the city around us.

I had a surprise planned for Christina, and after we finished our hot chocolate and scones, Angela returned her rent-a-bike and said she'd meet us back at the hotel. Christina and I set off on foot, heading toward the Claddagh store, where I had something special in mind. When we arrived, I bought her a Claddagh ring—her choice of style. It was a small gesture, but it meant a lot to me. A Claddagh ring, with its heart, hands, and crown, symbolizes love, friendship, and loyalty. The hands represent friendship, the heart stands for love, and the crown signifies loyalty. It's a beautiful symbol, and giving one to Christina felt right.

I was deeply grateful to her. She had set me on this path of travel and discovery, something I never imagined I'd do ever again, and for that, I would always be thankful. We both chose Claddagh rings as a token of our friendship, a reminder of this incredible journey we'd shared.

Tired and cold from the day's adventures, we made our way back to the hotel, ready to check in and rest, carrying with us not just the memories of the day but a lasting symbol of our bond.

On the way back to the hotel, we couldn't resist slipping into a cozy spot called Murty Rabbits, a traditional Irish pub that caught our attention with the lively sound of Irish music spilling out onto the street. Inside, the atmosphere was warm and inviting, with dark wood interiors and a bustling crowd enjoying the music. Behind the bar stood a bartender who was a dead ringer for Ed Sheeran—adorable and friendly, adding to the charm of the place.

We ordered pints of Guinness and settled in, chatting with some of the locals who were more than happy to share stories and make us feel welcome. The music, laughter, and richness of the pub made it feel like a quintessential Irish experience. After finishing our drinks, we reluctantly left the cheerful atmosphere behind and made our way to the hotel to find Angela, feeling content and connected to the vibrant spirit of Galway.

We arrived at the Eyre Square Hotel just as Angela was walking in—perfect timing. The staff, always friendly and efficient, retrieved our backpacks from a locked room, handed us our keys, and offered laundry service. They gave us labeled bags for our clothes, letting us know they'd be happy to wash them while we were out on tour the next day.

Our room was on the third floor—again! I was starting to sense a theme with this third-floor accommodation. After freshening up, we decided to head down to the hotel's restaurant for dinner.

Navigating the building was its own little adventure—thanks to Ireland's famously uneven flooring. First, we would need to go down three flights of stairs to the lobby, then descend another flight of stairs to reach the restaurant. If you needed the bathroom, that required yet another trip downstairs to the basement. All this walking was bound to get me in shape! But luckily, they did have an elevator, which we used a couple of times.

The restaurant at the Eyre Square Hotel was truly stunning, blending old-world charm with modern touches. The first thing that caught my eye was the rich, dark wood that made up the tables, bar, and paneling, all polished to a high shine that reflected the warm light from the chandeliers above. The chairs had a beautiful antique look, with intricate carvings and velvet cushions, but with a modern twist—rollers on the bottom, making them easy to move while keeping their classic elegance intact.

The walls were adorned with fancy, ornate paintings, each one adding a touch of sophistication to the space. Some depicted grand Irish landscapes, while others featured portraits that seemed to tell stories of a bygone era. The combination of the art, the gleaming wood, and the antique furniture gave the restaurant a timeless, almost regal feel. Yet, it was inviting and cozy, the perfect balance between elegance and comfort. It was easy to settle in and feel right at home while admiring the beauty around us.

I had been eagerly anticipating trying the fish and chips, and everything I'd read about Galway said that Galway was the place to do it. As I waited for my order, I could barely contain my excitement, my mind filled with high expectations. When the plate finally arrived, I was astonished by the sheer size of the fish. It was perfectly golden brown, crispy on the outside, and laid out on top of a generous bed of thick-cut chips. It looked absolutely mouthwatering!

The moment I took my first bite, I knew it lived up to the hype. The batter was light and crisp, with just the right amount of crunch, while the fish inside was tender, flaky, and full of flavor. It was, without a doubt, the best fish I'd ever eaten. Each bite was like a little piece of heaven, and I savored the balance of textures and flavors—delicate yet rich. The chips were equally delightful, crisp on the outside and soft on the inside, the perfect companion to the fish. It was the ultimate Galway experience, and I couldn't have been happier. Christina and I also decided to ask if they could make us our favorite drink, a Cucumber Chilton. Lo and behold, the bartender knew exactly what it was and was more than happy to make them.

We sat in the restaurant for a while, enjoying our food and Cucumber Chiltons while listening to Angela sharing the stories of her bike ride around Galway. Her adventures gave us a fresh perspective on the city. She mentioned the numerous Spanish flags flying in the Latin Quarter, something I hadn't noticed. She was excited to tell us about the vibrant streets and how the streets were alive with people from all over the world.

Angela had explored much more of Galway than we had, biking through quieter neighborhoods and along the waterfront, where the locals gathered to enjoy the fresh Atlantic breeze. She noticed the subtle blend of old and new—the way modern shops and cafes mingled with centuries-old stone buildings, many of which had been standing for generations. She described how Galway felt like a living, breathing place, with its own unique rhythm and sense of community, far beyond the usual tourist spots. Listening to her, I felt even more connected to the city, appreciating its deeper layers and the rich stories it held.

After finishing our meal, I thought we'd be calling it a night, heading up to the room for some rest. But Christina had other plans. She decided she wanted to go back to Murty Rabbits for another pint, and, with a mischievous grin, she trotted off to the pub on her own. A few minutes later, I decided to join her, curious to see what the night had in store.

As soon as I stepped outside the hotel, I could hear the music pouring out of Murty Rabbits, much louder than it had been earlier. The atmosphere had transformed completely. People were milling about outside, the air thick with conversation, laughter, and cigarette smoke. I made my way through the boisterous crowd, pushing through the haze of noise and energy until I spotted Christina inside. She was beaming, happily sipping her pint, and singing along with the rest of the crowd. The whole pub was packed and alive—traditional Irish tunes filled the air, and the energy was infectious.

I grabbed a pint and joined her, soaking in the electric atmosphere. The pub was completely full of people singing, laughing, and swaying to the music. It was a scene of pure joy, and we were fully swept up in it. After a few more pints, we decided it was time to head back to the hotel, and we wobbled our way up the street, still buzzing from the night's excitement. Thankfully, the hotel had an elevator because, after all that beer, climbing three flights of stairs would have been a challenge!

It was the perfect end to an exciting day in Galway—full of laughter, music, and great company. I couldn't have asked for a better way to wrap up our first night in this vibrant city.

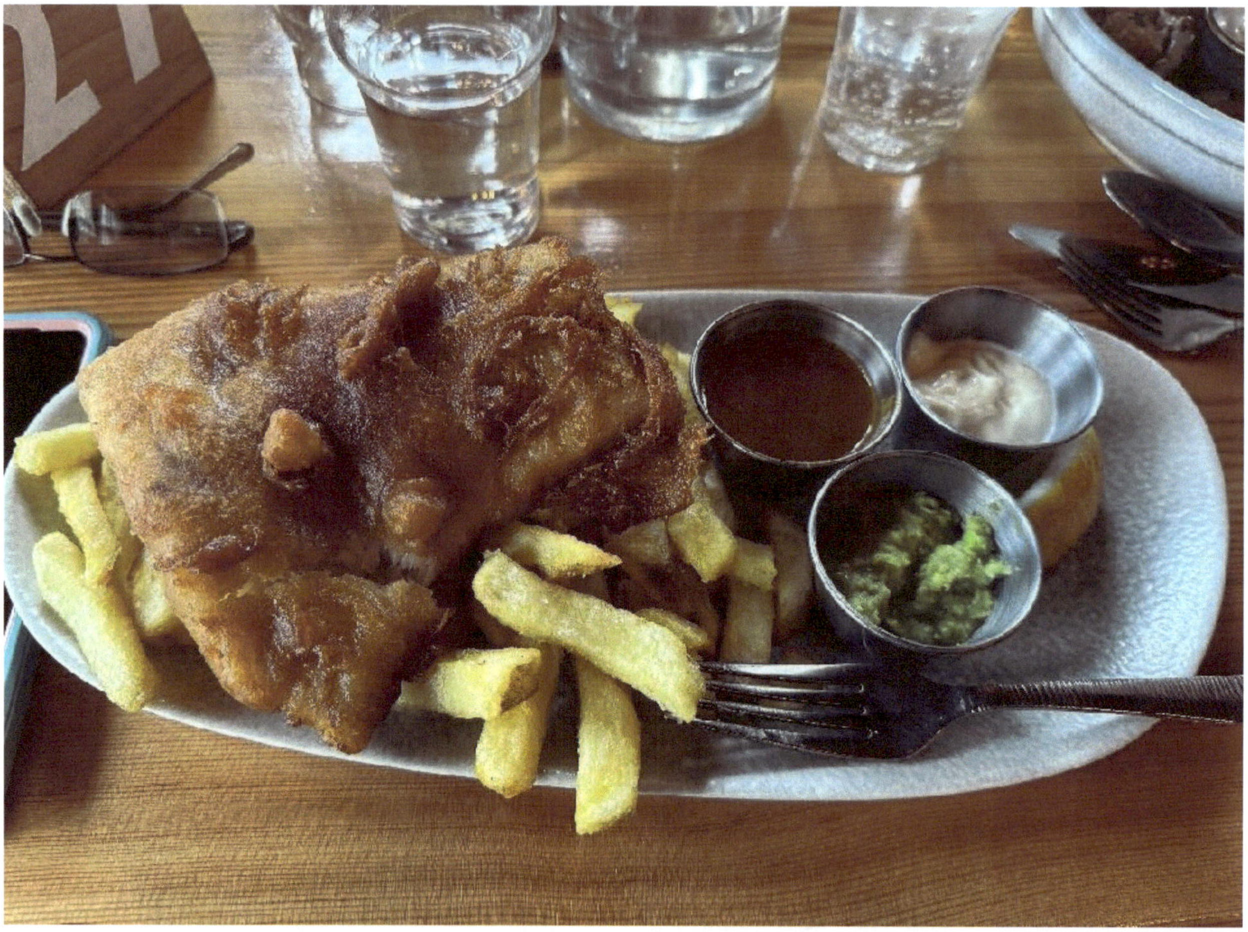

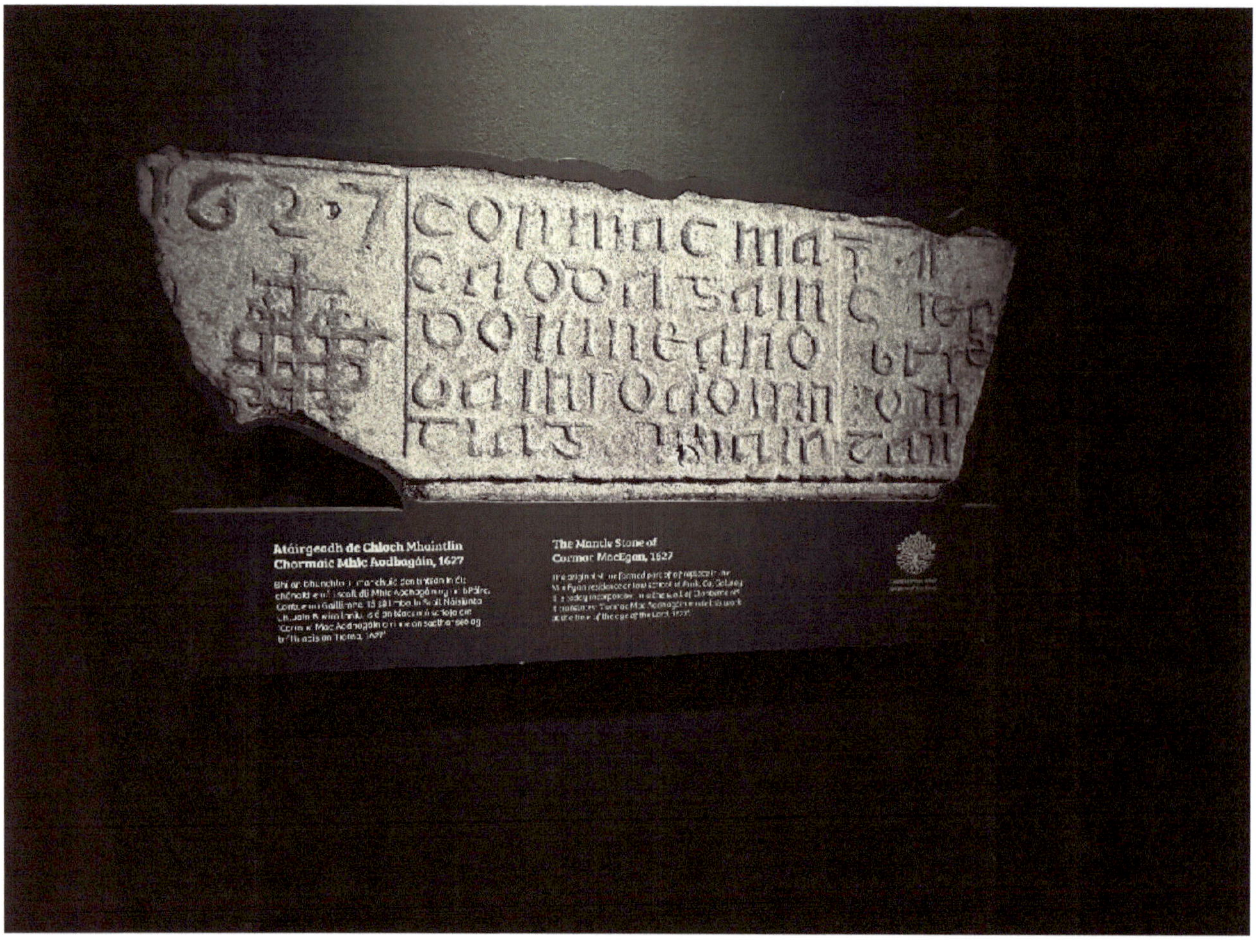
1627
Atáirgeadh de Chloch Mhaintlin
Chormaic Mhic Aodhagáin, 1627
The Mantle Stone of
Cormac MacEgan, 1627

CHAPTER EIGHT: CLIFFS OF MOHER

Day 6:

Day 6 began with an embarrassing moment that quickly turned into laughter. Angela and I woke up early and made our way down to the restaurant, waiting for Christina to join us. To get to the restaurant, we had to walk down a flight of stairs, and as luck would have it, I missed the last step and ended up faceplanting right in front of the entire room of early eaters.

The whole restaurant turned to look as I scrambled to my feet, feeling my face flush red. A waitress hurried over with a smile and thick Irish accent and said, "You took quite a tumble! Would you like me to make you a plate?" Trying to laugh off my embarrassment, I giggled and replied, "No thanks, I got me."

To recover from the moment, I decided to order a mimosa—with a double shot. It wasn't the most graceful start to the day, but we had a good laugh about it, and the humor set a lighthearted tone for the rest of the morning.

Shortly after, Christina joined us, and Angela wasted no time in recounting my little mishap. As soon as she finished the story, Christina burst out laughing, unable to contain herself. Hearing Angela's animated retelling, I couldn't help but laugh, too—it was impossible not to. What started as an embarrassing moment quickly became one of those memories we'd been laughing about for years.

After finishing our buffet breakfast, still chuckling, we headed to the pickup location for our next big adventure: The Cliffs of Moher! Excitement built as we set off, ready for another day of exploration and, hopefully, fewer faceplants.

While researching Ireland, one destination stood out above all others as a must-visit: the Cliffs of Moher. To make the trip unforgettable, I booked a tour with Wild Atlantic Way Day Tours, a company renowned for its excellent service and well-organized itineraries. The booking process was seamless, and their reputation gave me confidence in my choice. If you ever find yourself in Ireland and need a reliable tour company, I highly recommend Wild Atlantic Way Day Tours—they truly make exploring Ireland's iconic landscapes an exceptional experience.

We arrived at the pickup location for our Cliffs of Moher tour, and that's when we met our tour guide, Ian. He was the quintessential Irish jokester—exactly how I imagined all of Ireland to be! From the moment we stepped onto the bus, Ian kept us laughing with his quick wit and endless Irish humor. He had to be in his 60s, with a twinkle in his eye, and he couldn't stop bragging about his wife, a charming and wonderful Irish woman, as he described her. It was clear he adored her, and his stories had us all in stitches throughout the ride.

The tour bus was completely full, and I was fortunate to find a seat next to a charming young man from London. His British accent captivated me—I found myself hanging on to every word he said. What is it about the British accent that feels so commanding, professional, and intriguing?

He mentioned he was traveling alone and was excited to visit the Cliffs of Moher. He couldn't have been more than 35, and I was a bit surprised to learn he was exploring on his own. He explained that his girlfriend was also traveling solo but in South America. They certainly seemed like quite the adventurous couple!

Our first stop was Dunguaire Castle, a picturesque stone fortress that seemed to rise straight out of the misty landscape. The castle stood proudly on the shores of Galway Bay, its tall, gray stone tower surrounded by lush green grass. With its battlements and thick walls, you could imagine it standing strong through centuries of history, overlooking the water like a guardian of the coast. Ian had plenty of tales about the castle, each one more colorful than the last, adding even more laughter to the day.

Next, we stopped at a smaller version of the Cliffs of Moher, located in an area called the Burren. These cliffs were known as the Doolin Cliffs, and they were breathtaking. This unique landscape allowed us to get surprisingly close to the cliffs, which was both thrilling and a bit frightening. Angela, always the adventurer, got right up to the edge, which definitely spiked my anxiety, but she was having the time of her life, unfazed by the height or the drop below.

The weather had turned cooler, and a fine mist hung in the air, making everything feel fresh and a bit mysterious. We all had our jackets on, but the cold seemed secondary to the awe-inspiring views before us. The Burren itself was truly fascinating—unlike anything I had seen before. Its landscape is a vast, rocky terrain, almost otherworldly, with limestone pavements stretching out like natural stone pathways. The cliffs jutted out over the Atlantic Ocean, and the sound of the waves crashing below added to the dramatic effect.

The Burren is also home to rare plants and wildflowers that grow in the cracks between the rocks, making it one of Ireland's most unique ecosystems. Despite the cold, we were completely captured by the breathtaking beauty of the place. It felt like we had stepped into another world, one full of rugged cliffs and ancient landscapes, and it was an experience we wouldn't soon forget.

We boarded the bus and continued our journey toward the Cliffs of Moher, but not before Ian took us on a scenic drive through the village of Doolin. What a charming little town! Its brightly colored buildings and quaint shops lined the narrow streets, giving the place a whimsical, almost storybook feel. Though we didn't have time to get off the bus, we admired the vibrant houses and storefronts from our windows, each one painted in cheerful hues of pinks, blues, yellows, and greens.

Doolin is known for its traditional Irish music and cozy pubs, and I could easily imagine the lively atmosphere that fills the town in the evenings. Nestled in the heart of the countryside, with rolling green hills surrounding it, the town seemed like the perfect spot to escape the hustle and bustle of city life. The brief glimpse we had of Doolin left me wishing we could stay longer to explore, but our next destination awaited: the magnificent Cliffs of Moher.

When we arrived at the Cliffs of Moher, I quickly realized that no words could truly capture what lay before me. The cliffs were a testament to the raw power and beauty of Mother Nature—majestic and imposing, rising hundreds of feet above the Atlantic Ocean. The waves crashed relentlessly against the rocky shores below, their whitecaps a striking contrast to the deep blue of the sea. It was awe-inspiring.

The views were simply breathtaking. The cliffs stretched endlessly in both directions, their edges adorned with vivid green grass that clung precariously to the jagged rock as if it could slip and fall into the depths below at any moment. Seagulls and puffins darted through the air, their wings cutting effortlessly through the wind as they found their perches on the outcroppings jutting from the cliffs.

There was a solemn stillness in the air despite the constant roar of the ocean and the cries of the birds. Standing there, gazing out over the edge, I felt small in the face of such natural grandeur as though I were witnessing something ancient and eternal. The Cliffs of Moher weren't just a sight to see—they were an experience, a reminder of the untamed beauty of the world.

We began our visit to the Cliffs of Moher by exploring the museum, eager to absorb as much as we could about this incredible natural wonder. The museum offered fascinating insights into the history and geology of the cliffs, which have been sculpted by over 300 million years of natural forces. We learned that the cliffs stand as high as 700 feet at their tallest point and stretch for about 8 miles along the western coast of Ireland. The Cliffs of Moher are also home to a rich diversity of wildlife, including over 20 species of seabirds, with puffins being a particular highlight. The area has even been designated as a UNESCO Global Geopark, marking its global significance.

Armed with this knowledge, we headed outside to the walkway, where the real experience awaited us. The raw emotion hit immediately. Standing on the edge of the cliffs, we were met with sweeping views of the Atlantic Ocean, its waves pounding relentlessly against the rocky base below. The wind whipped around us, adding to the dramatic atmosphere, while the sheer drop of the cliffs made our hearts race with both awe and a sense of vulnerability. The landscape seemed to stretch endlessly, with the horizon blending seamlessly into the sky.

Every step along the walkway revealed new perspectives of the cliffs' rugged beauty. The scale was overwhelming, and it was easy to see why these cliffs have inspired legends and captured the imagination of visitors for centuries. Standing there, surrounded by the raw power of nature, it was impossible not to feel a deep connection to the land and the history that shaped it. The Cliffs of Moher weren't just a view—they were a profound, humbling experience.

Christina and I strolled along the long path that hugged the edge of the Cliffs of Moher. Angela, with her trusty binoculars in her hand, set off on a mission. She was determined to capture a picture of a puffin, and we happened to be there during their mating season—a prime time for viewing.

Hundreds of birds nested along the cliffs, attracting birdwatchers from all over the world, and Angela was no exception. Her passion for ornithology drove her determination, and she spent much of the tour scanning the cliffs and the sea with her binoculars, eager to spot one of these charming birds.

As we walked, she ventured off onto a separate, more daring path along the cliffs, one that gave her a better vantage point but was a bit more frightening due to the steep drops. She struck up conversations with fellow bird enthusiasts along the way, exchanging tips and hopes for a puffin sighting. Just when we thought time was running out and we'd have to head back to the bus, Angela managed to catch a glimpse of a puffin right before we were scheduled to leave. Her excitement was contagious, and it made her day.

For all of us, the entire experience at the Cliffs of Moher had been fulfilling in every possible way. The stunning views, the fresh sea air, and the joy of sharing these moments together made it a day to remember.

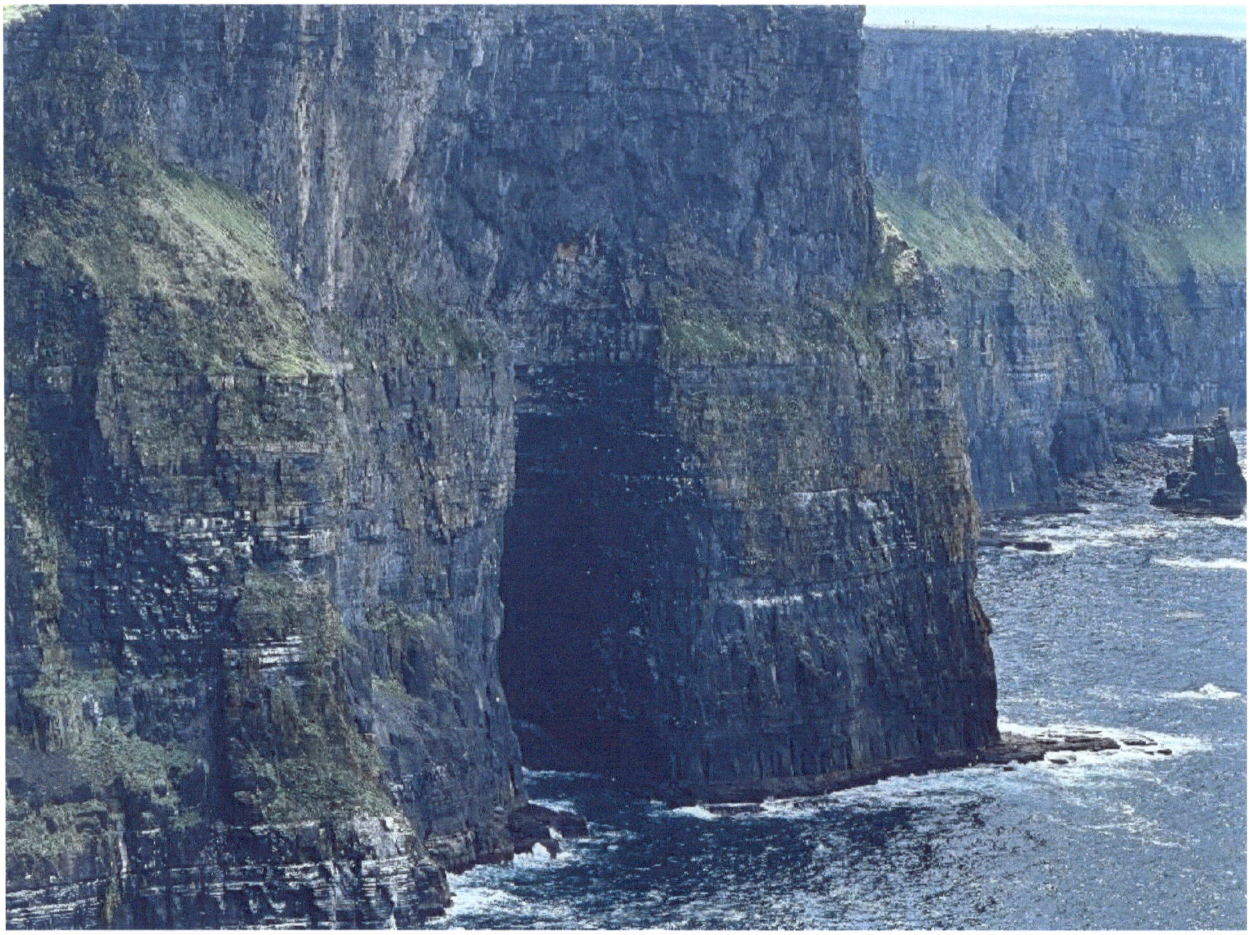

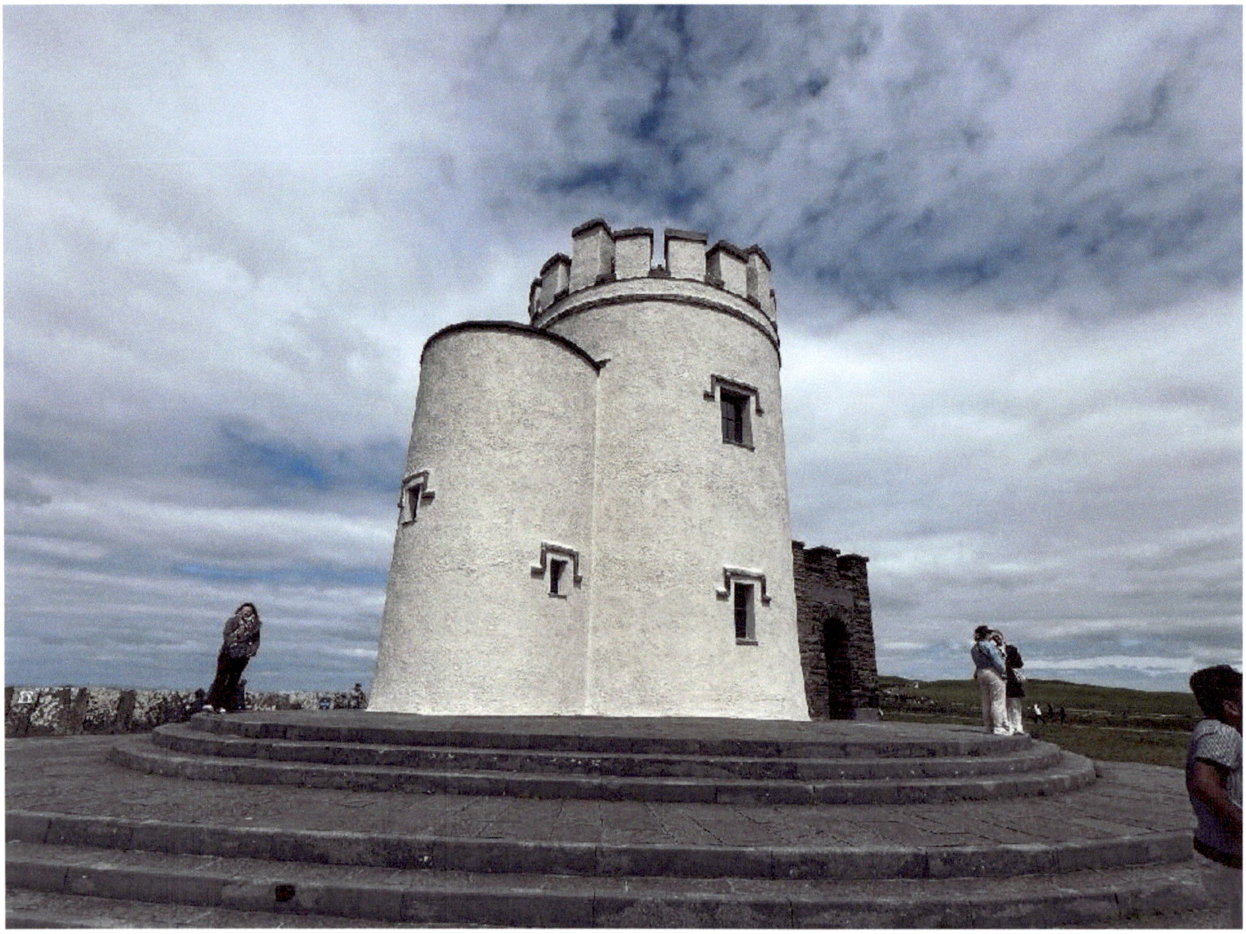

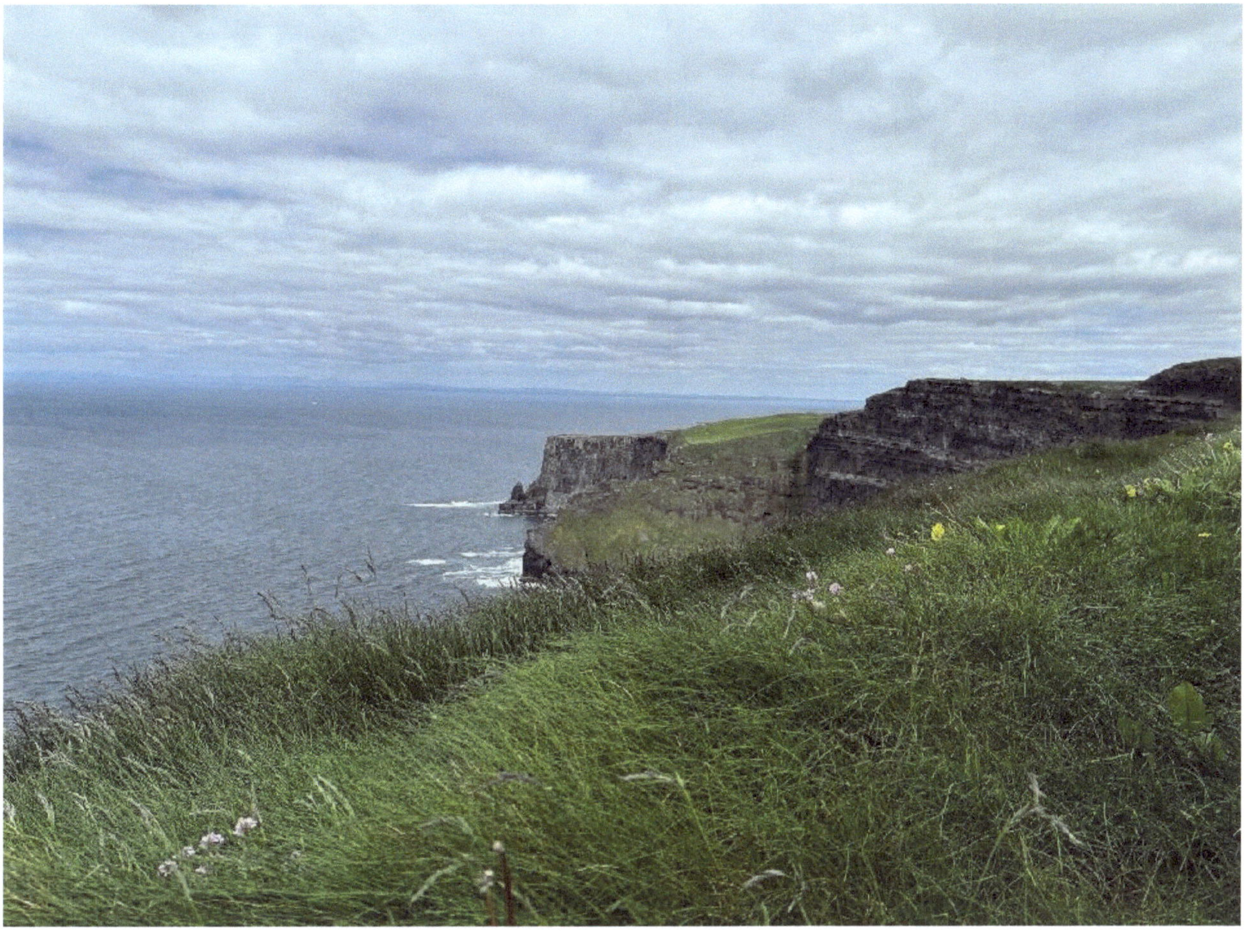

IN MEMORY OF THOSE WHO HAVE LOST
THEIR LIVES AT THE CLIFFS OF MOHER
I gcuimhne ar na daoine a
cailleadh ag Aillte an Mhothair

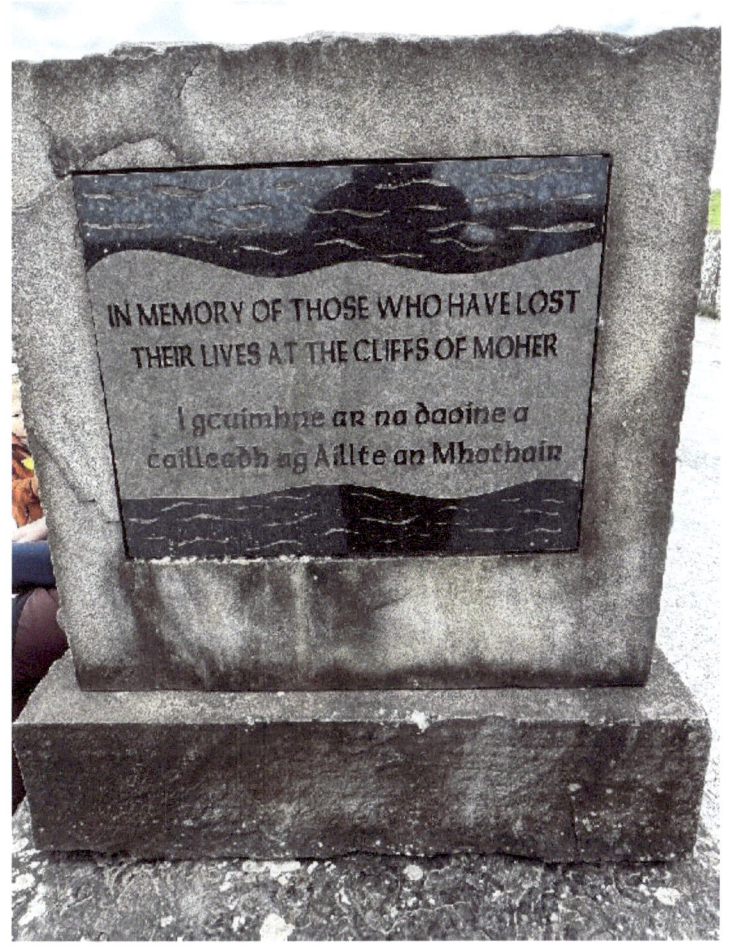

THE CLIFFS OF MOHER

Upon the edge of Ireland's west,

Where waves and wind never come to rest.

Stand the Cliffs of Moher,

So grand and alluring,

A natural wonder, ancient and enduring.

They rise from the sea,

A sheer wall of might.

Combined with the Green of Ireland's delight.

A history rich with tales untold,

Of battles so fierce and warriors so bold.

The Puffins dance on the breeze with ease,

Nature's chorus, wild and free.

A stunning beauty, raw and pure,

Mist kissed rocks, Ireland's allure.

Where emerald cliffs meet the pale blue sky,

You'll find a peace no money can buy.

I didn't want to leave, but it was time. As much as I wished to stay at the Cliffs of Moher, we had to head back. The ride back to Galway was filled with laughter, thanks to Ian's endless jokes, but there was also a sense of solemnity. The cliffs had left a deep impression on me, and I knew I would return someday.

By the time we arrived in Galway, we were all tired and hungry. We decided to head to the restaurant once again for a hearty meal and a couple of pints, reminiscing about the incredible day we'd had. I couldn't resist ordering the fish again, and once more, it was absolutely delicious. As we relaxed, the excitement of the day gradually faded into a peaceful contentment. Eventually, we made our way up to the room, ending the day with smiles on our faces and happiness in our hearts. It had been a day filled with beauty, adventure, and shared memories, the kind that would stay with us for a long time.

CHAPTER NINE: CORK

Day 7:

We got up early and enjoyed breakfast at the hotel, chatting about the four-hour train ride ahead to Cork. We knew we'd have to change trains twice along the way, but both stations were small, so we didn't expect any issues. After breakfast, we made the short walk to the train station, just a quick stroll from our hotel.

By the way, if you're ever in Galway and looking for a place to stay, I highly recommend the Eyre Square Hotel. It's truly one of the best accommodations I've experienced. The staff are incredibly friendly and always ready to help, the food and drinks are excellent, and they even offer free laundry service—a thoughtful touch that makes your stay even more convenient and enjoyable.

As we boarded the train, we struck up a conversation with a local man who shared his frustrations about Galway's rapidly growing population. He spoke about how the increasing crowds had changed the character of the city, making it feel busier and less intimate. While he wasn't thrilled with the congestion, he admitted that the population boom brought economic benefits through tourism and new businesses. It was fascinating to hear his perspective, though we couldn't help but wonder if he was subtly trying to make sure we weren't planning to stay long! Regardless, we were happy to listen and gain insight into the challenges locals face in a thriving, ever-evolving city like Galway. One of the great things about the Irish is that they aren't afraid to tell you what they think, and I, for one, loved it.

We settled into our seats on the train, ready for the long journey ahead, but the day quickly took a lively turn when we realized our section was filled with a group of young ladies on their way to Cork for a bachelorette party.

The bridesmaids had already started drinking and were having a blast. They were all dressed up, surrounded by balloons, signs, and everything needed for a party. The bride, having had a bit too much to drink the night before, was fast asleep for part of the ride, but the bridesmaids were in full swing. The energy in the car was off the charts, with champagne flowing and laughter echoing throughout. It was a sight to see them enjoying themselves so much, and their excitement was contagious.

By the time we reached our first train station to change trains, the bachelorette party was pretty well toasted. Strangely, they didn't board the second train with us. Maybe they had a change of plans, or they decided to take a different route, but the second leg of the trip was noticeably quieter and far less eventful. After all the commotion, the calm of the second train felt like a peaceful reset as we continued on our way to Cork.

The second train ride was brief, and soon, we found ourselves on the third and final train that would take us to Cork. With a bit of quiet time, I took the opportunity to write in my journal, reflecting on all the experiences we'd had so far. I realized how much I was truly enjoying myself. Ireland had exceeded my expectations—it was an incredible place, full of beauty, history, and endless things to do and see.

The people we met had been nothing but kind and welcoming, and I couldn't help but think back to some of the negative comments I'd seen on social media before the trip. I was so glad I hadn't let those opinions sway me. Every part of this journey had been fulfilling, and I hadn't encountered a single moment of ill will from anyone. Ireland was beyond what I had imagined, and I felt incredibly grateful to be here.

I thought the journey would feel longer, but between writing in my journal, socializing, and admiring the breathtaking scenery, time flew by. Before I knew it, the conductor announced that we were about 15 minutes from Cork. The excitement began to build as we prepared for our arrival.

When we finally pulled into the train station in Cork, we were amazed by how vibrant and beautiful the city looked. Everything was lush and green, and the streets were bustling with energy. We quickly grabbed a cab that took us to our final hotel of the trip—The Montenotte, a luxury hotel Christina had booked for us. As soon as we arrived, we were in awe of its beauty. The Montenotte was stunning, and we could already tell this would be the perfect place to end our adventure.

The Montenotte Hotel is a true gem in Cork, offering luxury and elegance in every corner. Perched on a hill, it boasts stunning panoramic views of the city, with its beautifully manicured gardens adding to the serene atmosphere. The moment we arrived, we were struck by the grandeur of the place. The exterior is modern yet charming, with large windows that let in plenty of natural light, and the lush greenery surrounding the hotel adds a sense of tranquility.

Stepping inside, the lobby exudes sophistication with its sleek design, plush seating, and tasteful décor. Everything about the Montenotte feels refined yet welcoming. The staff greeted us warmly, and the attention to detail in every aspect of the hotel was immediately apparent. The rooms are spacious and luxurious, with comfortable beds, high-end furnishings, and floor-to-ceiling windows that allow guests to soak in the views of Cork's skyline. The blend of contemporary design and cozy touches makes it feel like a true retreat.

The Montenotte also offers plenty of amenities to enhance your stay. There's a rooftop terrace that provides an incredible vantage point for watching the sunset over the city, a cinema room for private screenings, and a gorgeous indoor pool and spa area, perfect for unwinding after a day of exploring. The hotel's restaurant, Panorama Bistro & Terrace, is equally impressive, serving delicious meals made from fresh, local ingredients. Dining with a view of the city skyline is a highlight in itself.

Every detail of the Montenotte is designed to create a memorable and relaxing experience, from the beautifully landscaped gardens to the luxurious touches throughout the hotel.

Upon entering the hotel, we were greeted with warm smiles and a cheerful atmosphere. After checking in, we dropped our backpacks off in our beautiful room and headed straight down to the restaurant—we were starving! While waiting for a table, we ordered a couple of drinks, cranberry, and vodka this time, and decided to explore the grounds.

The gardens were magnificent, filled with vibrant flowers and perfectly manicured lawns. As we wandered through the beautifully landscaped paths, we stumbled upon a second bar—the very one we'd seen in pictures on social media. It was charming yet elegant, with a sleek wrap-around bar and colorful, stylish chairs that added a playful touch. The atmosphere was inviting, and we instantly knew this would be our post-dinner spot to relax.

We made a quick plan to head back to this delightful bar after our meal, where we could sit, unwind, and take in the view while soaking up the peaceful and elegant environment. It was the perfect way to continue our wonderful evening.

I decided to take a chance and ordered the fish and chips again, and once again, it did not disappoint. After a couple more cranberries and vodka, we wrapped up dinner and made our way to the second bar we had spotted earlier. Meanwhile, Angela had found another rent-a-bike location and was off on her own adventure, eager to explore everything Cork had to offer. I admired her ability to go exploring on her own. It takes a lot of courage to roam around a strange town in another country on your own.

Christina and I settled in at the second bar, enjoying the relaxed atmosphere and a couple of drinks. But it wasn't long before Angela called, excitedly inviting us to join her at a little bar she had discovered. Intrigued, we quickly finished our drinks, called a cab, and headed into downtown Cork to meet her.

As we wandered through the lively streets, we finally spotted the bar, its entrance marked by a vibrant mural of rainbow-colored wings painted on the outside wall. The clue was clear—this was a drag bar! To our surprise and excitement, the night was set for a big drag show event, and I couldn't wait to experience it. The energy in the air was infectious, and I knew it was going to be a night to remember.

I had been to one other drag show while visiting my son in Phoenix, and it was such a fun experience, so I was excited to see another one here in Cork. This show did not disappoint! The performers were dressed to the nines in elaborate dresses, their makeup flawless, and their voices were spot-on as they belted out classic songs that had the whole crowd singing along. The energy in the room was electric, packed with young people enjoying the lively atmosphere.

Christina and Angela, full of excitement, made their way up to the stage during intermission, dancing with a few other patrons. It was a joy to watch them, mother and daughter, mingling with the crowd and embracing the fun. After the show, and with a few more drinks in our system, we stumbled out of the bar, laughing and happy, and made our way back to the hotel to call it a night. It had been such a wonderful experience, full of vibrant energy and great company.

CHAPTER TEN: BLARNEY CASTLE

Day 8:

Day 8 began with a hearty breakfast from the impressive spread in the hotel restaurant. The coffee was absolutely to die for—though, to be fair, the added Baileys might have had something to do with that! One thing that struck me as peculiar was the absence of potatoes. I mean, wasn't Ireland famous for its potatoes? I couldn't help but wonder what was up with that.

I also asked for milk with my coffee, and our waiter brought out little packets of milk—just like the ketchup or mustard packets we get in the States. It was definitely different but charming in its own way. The china they used was delicate and dainty, adding an elegant touch to the meal.

It rained all day, which felt unusual to us since we were from the desert Southwest of the States, but I didn't mind at all. In fact, I love the rain—I'd happily live anywhere that had frequent rainy days. After breakfast, we caught an Uber and headed off to Blarney Castle, a destination that's very popular in the States and one that had long been at the top of my bucket list. The excitement of finally visiting this iconic place made the rainy weather seem like a perfect backdrop for the day ahead.

Blarney Castle was absolutely breathtaking. The lush, green landscape stretched out in every direction, with beautifully manicured gardens that seemed to go on forever. We spent at least two hours wandering through the vibrant gardens, which were filled with an incredible variety of flowers, trees, and bushes, some of which I had never seen before. The colors were stunning—bright bursts of reds, yellows, and purples set against the rich green foliage. Every corner we turned revealed something new, from hidden pathways to peaceful ponds and even some whimsical sculptures dotted throughout the grounds.

The gardens themselves are famous, particularly the Poison Garden, which showcases plants known for their toxic properties, all carefully labeled with fascinating information. There's also the Fern Garden and the Rock Close, with their ancient stones and mystical atmosphere, adding a layer of enchantment to the already magical setting.

After soaking in the gardens' beauty, we made our way to the castle itself. Blarney Castle, with its towering stone walls and centuries-old charm, stood majestically in the middle of the estate.

Steeped in history and legend, the castle has long been a symbol of Ireland's rich heritage. We were excited to explore the interior and, of course, to visit the famous Blarney Stone—a bucket-list item for many, including myself.

I was absolutely determined to kiss the famous Blarney Stone, but we quickly learned that getting to the top of the castle wouldn't be as easy as we'd thought. The climb involved navigating narrow, winding stone steps that had been there for hundreds of years. Some of the steps were uneven and steep, making the ascent feel a bit dangerous, but we carefully followed the line of visitors ahead of us, step by step.

As we climbed, I found myself thinking about the history etched into the worn stone beneath my feet— the tales of knights, poets, and dreamers who had walked this same path over the centuries. The air inside the castle was cool and damp, carrying an eerie feeling of ancient times. Occasionally, rays of sunlight pierced through the narrow slats in the stone walls, casting long shadows in the dimly lit spaces. Every corner seemed to hold secrets, and I couldn't help but wonder about the countless people who had made this climb before us. What thoughts had crossed their minds as they made their way to the top, just as we were now? It was both a thrilling and reflective experience, knowing we were part of a long line of history in this storied place.

The Blarney Stone is one of Ireland's most famous landmarks. The stone itself is embedded in the battlements of the castle, and according to legend, kissing it grants the "gift of eloquence" or the ability to speak with charm and persuasion—what is often referred to as "blarney."

The exact origins of the Blarney Stone are steeped in myth and mystery, with several tales surrounding how it came to be placed in the castle. One popular story suggests that the stone was a gift from the goddess Clíodhna to Cormac MacCarthy, the Lord of Blarney, in gratitude for his help in a legal matter. Another tale ties the stone to the Stone of Scone, used in the coronation of Scottish kings, though this has not been historically verified. Some legends even claim it was part of the Stone of Jacob, which biblical figures used as a pillow.

The term "blarney" itself dates back to the 16th century. It is said that Queen Elizabeth I coined the term when dealing with Cormac MacCarthy, who used flattering words and diplomatic delays to avoid surrendering his castle to English rule. Frustrated by his sweet-talking but unyielding behavior, the queen reportedly remarked that his promises were "all Blarney," meaning they were eloquent but deceptive.

Kissing the Blarney Stone has been a tradition for centuries, with visitors from all over the world climbing to the top of the castle to take part in the ritual. The act of kissing the stone isn't as straightforward as it sounds—visitors must lean backward while holding onto iron rails and arch themselves over a gap to reach the stone. Despite the awkward position, people from all walks of life, including famous figures like Winston Churchill, have made the climb to kiss the stone in hopes of gaining the gift of eloquence.

We finally reached the top of the castle, an area known as the battlements. I was up first. Bending backward, I carefully lowered myself down to the Blarney Stone and gave it a big kiss. I heard the click of the camera and was relieved to pull myself back up—it was a little nerve-wracking to lean over like that, hanging backward over the edge just to reach the stone.

Next, it was Christina's turn. She followed suit, leaning back and lowering herself to kiss the stone. Just as she straightened back up, her phone rang—it was Angela, calling to let us know she had decided to climb the stairs and kiss the stone, too. So, we waited at the top of the castle, and soon enough, Angela arrived and took her turn, kissing the stone with as much determination as we had.

The views from the top of the castle were absolutely breathtaking. Standing there, I felt transported back in time, imagining myself centuries ago, watching an invading army approaching in the distance. The majesty of the place, combined with the sense of history it carried, was humbling. The castle's commanding presence and the stunning views left me in awe, surrounded by both beauty and the weight of the past.

After we had all kissed the Blarney Stone, it was time to make our descent. We took a different set of narrow stone steps down to the bottom of the castle, arriving at an area called the hearth. The atmosphere was a bit eerie as we wandered through the various empty rooms, each one silent and filled with the weight of history.

In the main hearth area, there was a large open space where fires were once used for cooking and warmth. I couldn't imagine living in such a place—the fire would have provided some heat, but the dampness in the air must have been ever-present, making it feel cold and uncomfortable. We passed through several rooms, including one marked as the "children's room," a reminder of the lives that once filled this castle. The entire experience left me reflecting on what life might have been like within these stone walls, where history felt so tangible, and the past seemed to linger in every corner.

We took our time, stopping to read each sign and description as we explored the castle. One sign, in particular, caught our attention—it was labeled "Murder Hole." Intrigued but slightly unsettled, we realized we'd have to climb back up the stone steps to about the third floor to see it for ourselves.

Once there, we discovered that the murder hole was positioned directly above the main entrance of the castle. Its purpose was grim: during an attack, defenders would pour hot oil or other deadly substances down onto anyone attempting to breach the doors. It gave us all a bit of a creepy feeling, knowing how such brutal tactics were used to defend the castle in its time. The history here was fascinating, but this particular detail really drove home the harsh realities of life in a fortress during those times.

We descended once again and found ourselves back in the main living area of the castle. We stopped to examine the massive fireplace, which spanned an entire wall. I couldn't imagine how much wood it would take to keep a place like this warm, but given the surrounding forest, I'm sure they had plenty of it. Perhaps the stones absorbed the heat after a fire burned for a while, helping to keep the castle somewhat warm.

As I stood there, thinking about how the castle might have been heated in those days, a sudden chill ran through me. Whether it was the thought of the cold, damp stone walls or the steady rain now dripping in through the open top of the castle, I felt the cold in my bones. It was a haunting reminder of how different life must have been for those who lived within these ancient walls.

We finally made our way back out onto the castle grounds and decided to warm up with a hot drink. An old stable from the 1800s had been converted into a cozy coffee shop and lunch area, so we headed inside. We ordered hot chocolate and scones, then sat in one of the stables to enjoy our treats. It was definitely a unique experience, sitting in what was once a place for horses, now transformed into a charming little café.

The rain continued to pour down, and as it didn't seem like it was going to let up anytime soon, we decided to head back into the shop to buy some umbrellas. It was clear we'd need them for the rest of the day!

With umbrellas in hand, we ventured down a path to see what else the grounds of Blarney Castle had to offer. As we walked, we came across a sign that read "Druid Cave," piquing our curiosity. Intrigued, we slipped through an opening in the rock fence and followed the path deeper into the grounds.

The atmosphere changed as we entered the area, which felt mystical and ancient. Large stones, known as Druid Stones, were scattered throughout, their placement hinting at the sacred rituals that might have taken place there centuries ago. The cave itself was a small, dark opening in the rock, almost hidden among the overgrown greenery. It was easy to imagine ancient Druids using this secluded spot for ceremonies or seeking refuge.

The cave's interior was cool and damp, with the air thick with a sense of history. It was a quiet, reflective space, and standing there, it felt like stepping back in time. The combination of the stones, the cave, and the steady rain added to the mysterious and enchanting feeling of the place, making it one of the more magical moments of our visit.

After making our way back to the main path, we decided to head toward Blarney Lake. The walk was long, winding around the lake's edge, but it felt utterly enchanting. The rain continued to fall steadily, and I quickly realized that my jacket wasn't as waterproof as I had thought. A chill began to creep in, but I was so captivated by the beauty of the area that I barely noticed it.

As we walked, we stumbled upon a small side path that led to an old boat dock. Grateful for a break from the rain, we sat there for a while, taking in the peaceful scene before us. Ducks floated lazily by on the lake's surface, and from our spot, we could see the silhouette of the castle in the distance, framed by the misty rain. The atmosphere was tranquil, almost otherworldly.

Eventually, with the rain still falling steadily, we knew we couldn't stay sheltered forever, so we decided to continue our walk. Along the path, we noticed how moss seemed to cover everything. The thick, green carpet clung to rocks, trees, and even the ground, soft and springy to the touch. I couldn't get over how the moss seemed to thrive in every nook and cranny, adding to the lush, magical feel of the area. Despite the rain and the damp chill, the walk around Blarney Lake was mesmerizing, as if nature itself was alive with history and charm.

We continued our walk around the lake and soon passed a small stone cottage with a charming thatched roof. It was like something straight out of a storybook, embodying the Ireland I had always imagined. The rain continued to fall steadily as if Ireland itself was showing us why its landscapes are so famously green.

We walked through dense forests, surrounded by greenery so lush it almost felt unreal. The air was thick with the earthy smell of wet leaves and damp soil, filling our senses with the essence of nature. The rain danced across the surface of the lake, creating gentle ripples as if each droplet was performing its own delicate dance. In some spots, the leaves fell softly from the trees, adding a peaceful rhythm to the moment, almost as if nature itself was breathing in harmony with us.

There was a deep connection to the earth in those moments—the steady rainfall, the whispers of the wind, and the sense of being cradled by nature. As we walked, it felt as though the whispers of ancestors guided our steps, leading us back to the castle we had left just hours earlier. It was a truly magical experience, connecting us to both the land and the history that surrounds it.

The last leg of the walk turned into an unexpected comedy show. The wind picked up, and suddenly, Christina's umbrella gave out, with half of it collapsing straight onto her face. She tried valiantly to fight against the wind and see where she was going, but it was a losing battle. The umbrella had practically wrapped itself around her head, making it impossible to use.

Determined not to be defeated, she grabbed the end of the umbrella and stretched her arm out, using it like an anchor to keep the thing from flapping back into her face. The sight of her wrestling with the umbrella, the wind blowing it every which way, had us in stitches. We couldn't stop laughing at the comical scene of her battling the elements, umbrella flapping wildly as she marched on. It was pure slapstick, and even Christina couldn't help but laugh at her own ridiculous struggle!

We finally made it back to the horse stalls-turned-coffee shop and decided to grab another hot chocolate to warm ourselves up. Christina wasted no time tossing her broken umbrella into the trash and happily started sipping her drink. Despite the rain and wind, it had truly been a wonderful day.

After finishing our hot chocolate, we wandered over to the gift shop near the entrance, browsing through the trinkets and souvenirs. We picked up a few mementos before calling a cab to take us back to The Montenotte.

Reflecting on the day, it had been an incredible experience—one where we were fully in tune with Mother Nature. The beauty of Blarney, the adventure through rain-soaked paths, and the laughter shared made it unforgettable.

When we arrived back at The Montenotte, we headed upstairs to change into dry clothes. Once we were warm and comfortable, we set off for another restaurant Christina had found, Gallagher's. Having tried most of the items on my Irish food list, I decided to go with Irish stew this time, especially since it was a cold and wet day.

Gallaghers did not disappoint. The savory smells wafting from the front door made me even hungrier, especially after the long walk at Blarney Castle. I was ready for a hearty meal, and when the Irish stew arrived, it was more like a pot pie—and incredibly delicious. The dish came with real mashed potatoes, beautifully presented with decorative waves on top. Paired with a hearty pint of Guinness, the meal was everything I'd hoped for.

We raised our glasses, toasting to a perfect day with a cheerful "Sláinte!" like they do in Ireland. After finishing up, we made our way back to The Montenotte for one last night in Cork, satisfied, tired, and happy from a wonderful day.

CHAPTER ELEVEN: SAYING GOODBYE

Day 9:

Day 9 was our final day in Ireland, and I knew I would miss this wonderful place and its people. Speaking of people, we had the most wonderful waiter during our stay at The Montenotte—his name was Matteo. He was incredibly attentive and kind and made sure all our needs were met. We were so impressed with his service that we all wrote glowing reviews for him on the hotel's website.

Here's what I wrote:

"*Matteo is a fantastic addition to your staff. He was extremely kind and attentive, always professional yet friendly. My experience at The Montenotte was delightful from the moment we arrived. The warm and inviting atmosphere set the tone for our two-night stay. Matteo was the most attentive waiter we had, and he truly made an impression. His genuine kindness and impeccable service elevated our dining experience. Matteo has a charming demeanor that instantly puts us at ease. Matteo, if you're reading this, keep spreading that kindness and warmth—it truly makes a difference.*"

It was a heartfelt goodbye not only to Matteo but also to the unforgettable memories of Cork, Ireland.

We packed up our suitcases, struggling to fit in all the gifts we had bought for friends and family, and headed out the door toward the train station for our journey back to Dublin. Our flight was scheduled for 1 pm, and we had plenty of time. As we walked, I couldn't help but feel the sadness creeping in, knowing that our time in Ireland was coming to an end.

Though I was certainly sad to be leaving, I was also incredibly grateful for the experience. Ireland had been so welcoming, full of warmth, and home to some of the most breathtaking views I had ever seen. As I reflect on this trip, I will now call it my "Emerald Journey" because this beautiful island truly lived up to its name. Ireland will always hold a special place in my heart, and I know I'll return someday.

I would be remiss if I didn't finish this book with a recap of all of our experiences.

As I sit back at home, flipping through photos of Ireland, I realize Ireland wasn't just a destination; it was a rekindling of joy and wonder. We felt the soul of Ireland in every moment of our journey. In Dublin, the lively Irish music coursed through our bones and hearts, filling us with energy and joy. In Galway, the ocean breeze kissed our faces, carrying with it the unmistakable taste of freedom and wonder. And in Cork, happiness and kindness seemed to radiate from every corner, wrapping us in the warmth of its people. Each place reminded us of the magic that is uniquely Ireland.

The fish and chips were unparalleled. They were so delicious and satisfying that we had them numerous times, and each meal felt like discovering a new kind of perfection.

At the ancient monolithic sites and towering castles, history came alive. We could feel the echoes of a thousand years and were transported back in time, standing where others once stood, dreaming their dreams. Exploring Ireland's folklore and legends around its ancient sites was nothing short of mind-boggling. Each story felt like a portal to another realm, connecting the past to the present in a way that was both mystical and humbling.

The smell of freshly baked scones mingled with the steam of hot chocolate, comforting us in a way only Ireland could. Every sip of Guinness carried the essence of Ireland's heart, deep and rich, served with pride in every bar.

Whether by train or car, every journey revealed a scenic view that felt like stepping into a postcard. No place could compare to the rolling green hills, the rugged cliffs, or the serenity of the countryside. And despite my initial worries, the transportation was surprisingly seamless—user-friendly and reliable, leaving me wondering why I had ever been anxious in the first place.

Ireland reminded me of home in many ways. The people have a fierce devotion to their country, yet they carry it with humility and kindness that feels genuine and heartfelt.

The photos I'd seen online didn't even come close to capturing the beauty—not just of the landscapes but of the people and their spirit.

Before this trip, I'll admit I was apprehensive. My research had uncovered stories of some Irish folks who weren't particularly fond of Americans, and I braced myself for the possibility of cold encounters. But once I arrived, all those worries melted away. Everywhere we went, we were met with warmth and friendliness. Strangers became conversationalists, and their openness was as disarming as it was delightful.

The Irish people weren't just polite; they were genuinely interested. They'd chat endlessly, sharing stories and laughs, until you were the one who had to excuse yourself to move on. It was a kind of hospitality that felt effortless, a natural extension of who they were.

Ireland wasn't just a beautiful destination—it was a reminder that kindness transcends borders and that, sometimes, reality can exceed even the highest expectations.

If I could offer any advice to future travelers, it would be this: relax and fully embrace Ireland. Don't stress about a thing while you're here—the people are incredibly kind and always willing to lend a hand if any issues arise. The hotel staff are some of the friendliest you'll ever encounter, and their warmth will make you feel right at home.

Don't be startled if a stranger strikes up a conversation; it's just part of the Irish charm. Embrace it—it's these unexpected moments that make the experience unforgettable. And whatever you do, visit as many pubs as you can. They're vibrant, full of life and laughter, and the perfect place to soak in the local culture.

Don't hesitate to ask for something out of the ordinary; the Irish will do their best to accommodate you. But remember, you're here to experience *their* way of life, so step out of your comfort zone. Try the food, savor the drinks, and let loose—you're in a place that celebrates living.

The people of Ireland are among the greatest you'll ever meet, and you'd truly miss out if you didn't take the time to connect with them. Every encounter, every smile, and every story add to the magic of this incredible country.

Goodbye Ireland!
See you soon!

ACROSS THE SEA

Before I journeyed across the sea,
I braced for cold hostility.
An American heart in a foreign land,
Expecting silence, a withdrawn hand.

But Ireland greeted me, warm and kind,
With open hearts and open minds.
Laughter spilled from every face,
In this green and storied place.

As I roamed its hills and skies,
I saw a truth before my eyes.
America and Ireland, worlds apart,
Share freedom's fire within the heart.

Together we've fought for common goals,
For liberty's light, for human souls.
Our histories ring with battles won,
United beneath the burning sun.

And now, as I leave, my heart feels torn,
For the land that embraced me, where memories were born.
I will always recall your kindness and grace,
The magic of every treasured place.

I know in my heart I'll return one day,
To wander your shores and hear your songs play.
Ireland, you're more than a journey, you're a part of me,
A bond eternal, across the sea.

www.ingramcontent.com/pod-product-compliance
Lightning Source LLC
Chambersburg PA
CBHW041550120626
46551CB00002B/166